# dk online

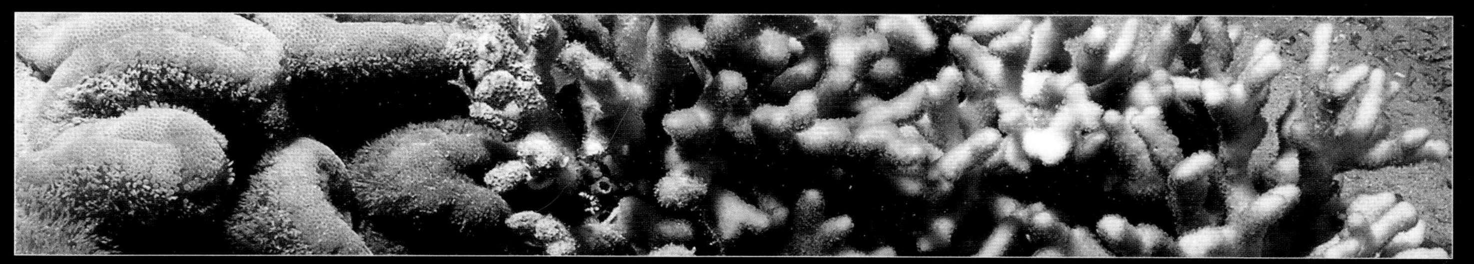

# oceans

London, New York, Melbourne,
Munich, and Delhi

**Project Editor** Ankush Saikia
**Editors** Aakriti Singhal, Pankhoori Sinha
**Senior Editors** Claire Nottage, Shaila Brown
**Weblink Editors** Steve Carton, Niki Foreman, Roger Brownlie

**Managing Editor** Linda Esposito

**Jacket Copywriter** Adam Powley
**Jacket Editor** Mariza O'Keeffe

**Publishing Manager** Andrew Macintyre
**Category Publisher** Laura Buller

**Consultant** Professor Dorrik Stow, University of Southampton

**Art Director** Shefali Upadhyay
**Project Art Editor** Kavita Dutta
**Designers** Mahua Mandal, Neerja Rawat
**Senior Art Editor** Jacqui Swan

**Managing Art Editor** Diane Thistlethwaite

**Jacket Manager** Sophia M Tampakopoulos Turner
**Jacket Designer** Neal Cobourne

**DTP Coordinator** Sunil Sharma
**DTP Designer** Harish Aggarwal

**Picture Research** Kate Lockley
**Picture Librarian** Rose Horridge
**Production** Erica Rosen

First published in the United States in 2008
by Dk Publishing, 375 Hudson Street, New York, New York, 10014

08 09 10 11 12 10 9 8 7 6 5 4 3 2 1
ED594–15/11


Published in Great Britain by Dorling Kindersley Limited.

A catalog record for this book is available from the Library of Congress.

ISBN: 978-0-7566-3462-9 (Paperback)
ISBN: 978-0-7566-3463-6 (Hard cover)

Color reproduction by Colourscan, Singapore
Printed in China by Toppan Printing Co. (Shenzen) Ltd.

Discover more at
**www.dk.com**

dkonline

# Oceans

Written by John Woodward

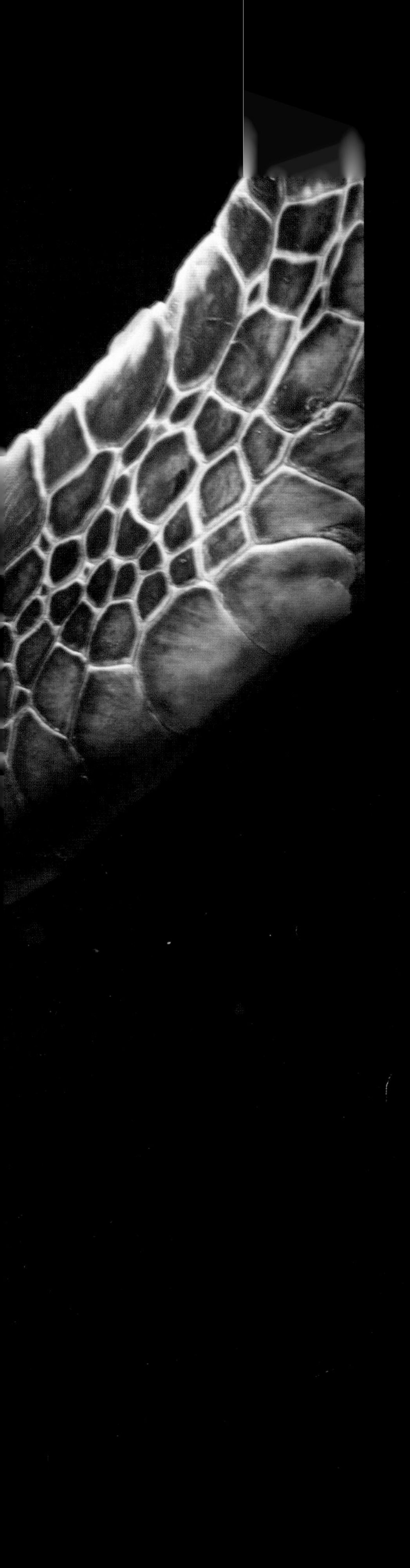

# CONTENTS

# How to use the dk online website

*dk online oceans* has its own website, created by DK and Google™. When you look up a subject in the book, the article gives you key facts and displays a keyword that links you to extra information online. Just follow these easy steps.

## http://www.oceans.dkonline.com

**Enter this website address...**

http://www.oceans.dkonline.com

**Find the keyword in the book...**

You can use only the keywords from the book to search on our website for the specially selected DK/Google links.

**Enter the keyword...**

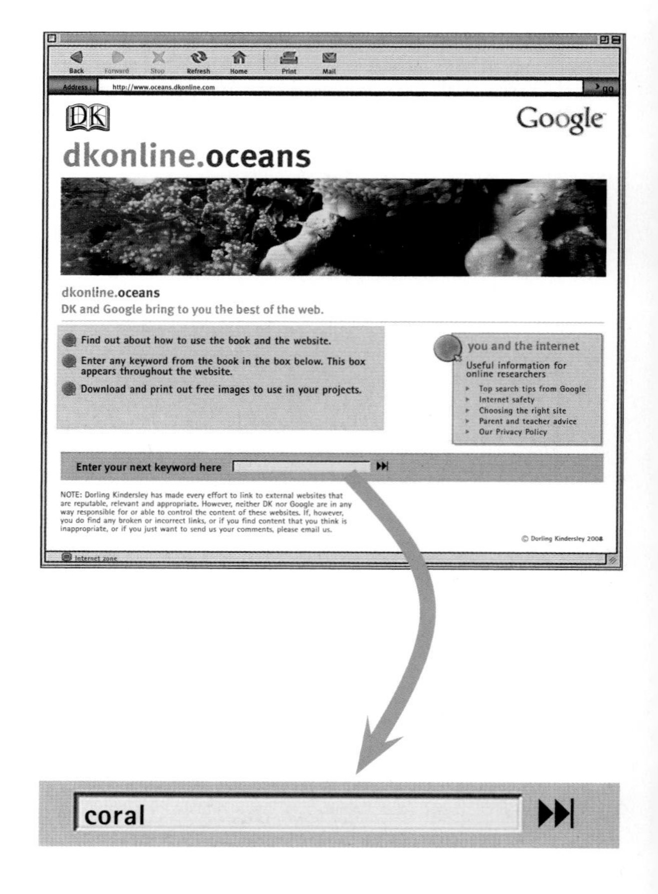

## Be safe while you are online:

- Always get permission from an adult before connecting to the internet.
- Never give out personal information about yourself.
- Never arrange to meet someone you have talked to online.
- If a site asks you to log in with your name or email address, ask permission from an adult first.
- Do not reply to emails from strangers—tell an adult.

**Parents:** Dorling Kindersley actively and regularly reviews and updates the links. However, content may change. Dorling Kindersley is not responsible for any site but its own. We recommend that children are supervised while online, that they do not use Chat Rooms, and that filtering software is used to block unsuitable material.

## 4 Click on your chosen link...

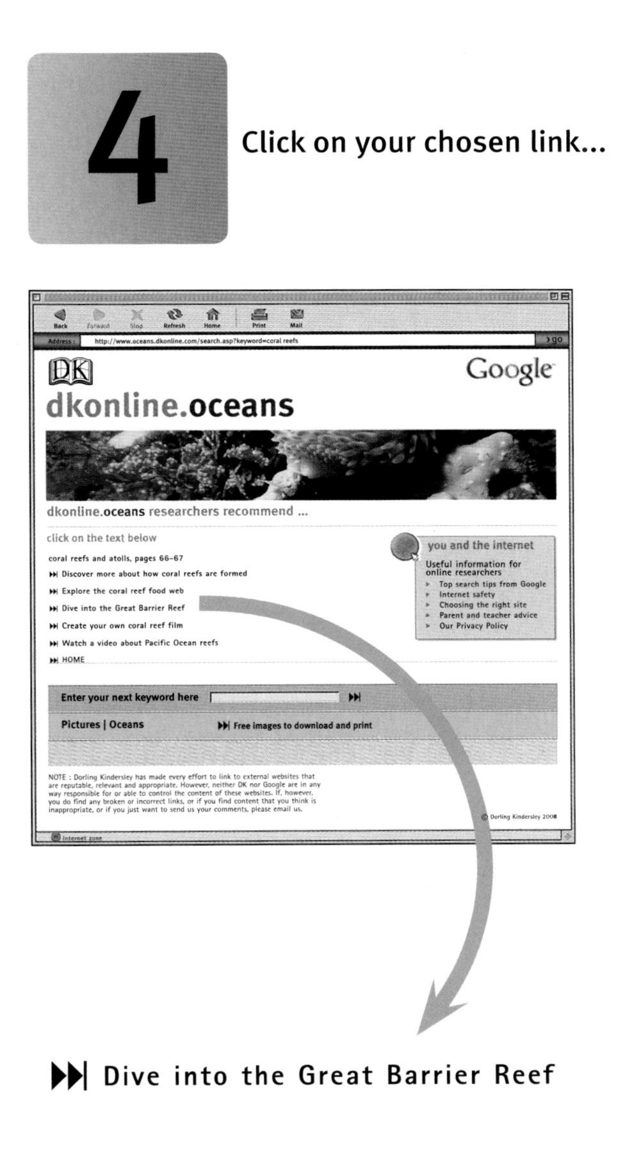


▶▶| Dive into the Great Barrier Reef

Links include animations, videos, sound buttons, virtual tours, interactive quizzes, databases, timelines, and realtime reports.

## 5 Download fantastic pictures...

The pictures are free of charge, but can be used for personal, noncommercial use only.

**Go back to the book for your next subject...**

# AN OCEAN PLANET

Planet Earth is really a planet of oceans. They cover more than two-thirds of its surface, to an average depth of 2.4 miles (3.8 km), making them the Earth's dominant environment. It is the only planet in the solar system that has liquid oceans, and it is no coincidence that it is the only planet known to support life. Water is vital to all forms of life, and it is likely that life on Earth began in the oceans. Oceans also make life on land possible, so without them humans could not exist.

▲ IDEAL SITUATION
Earth's oceans exist due to a combination of lucky circumstances. The planet's distance from the Sun creates ideal temperatures that allow water to exist as a liquid. Its size and gravity enable it to retain an atmosphere of air and water vapor. This acts as insulation, and stops the oceans from boiling away or freezing solid.

## OTHER WORLDS

MERCURY
The closest planet to the Sun, Mercury is much smaller than Earth. It does not have enough gravity to retain an insulating atmosphere, so its temperature fluctuates from -292°F (-180°C) to 806°F (430°C) and it is just a barren rocky sphere.

VENUS
Nearly the same size as Earth, Venus has enough gravity to retain a thick atmosphere. But this is mostly carbon dioxide, which traps the Sun's heat and creates searing surface temperatures of up to 930°F (500°C).

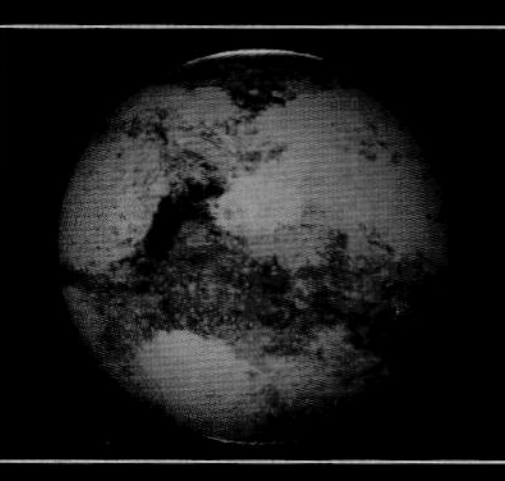

MARS
Too small to have more than a thin atmosphere, Mars is also colder than Earth because it is farther away from the Sun. Mars does have some water, but this is frozen into ice at its poles and beneath its surface, so the water does not form oceans.

EUROPA
One of the moons of Jupiter, Europa is rocky with a surface of solid ice, but it is possible that there is liquid water beneath the ice. If so, it might be the only other planet in the solar system that has extensive water, and a chance of supporting life.

▲ DEEP BLUE
The oceans have a total volume of about 319 million cubic miles (1,330 million cubic km). This is about a thousand times the volume of land above sea level. Living things can occupy all this space, and not just live on or near the surface as they do on land. So the total living space in the oceans is colossal, making them the most important habitat for life on Earth.

ocean planet

▲ TROPICAL SEAS
The world's oceans include a variety of environments. At one extreme, the warm, clear surface waters of the tropics support a dazzling variety of life, but often in small numbers because the clear waters contain very little food.

▲ ICY OCEANS
At the other extreme, surface waters near the poles freeze over for much of the year. Only a few types of animals can cope with this, but they can form huge populations because the cool, cloudy waters are rich in food resources.

## THE WORLD'S OCEANS

The world's oceans are separated by the continents into five main oceans, with the Atlantic, Pacific, and Indian Ocean linked in the south by the Southern Ocean. Each ocean has its own character, but water constantly flows from one to another.

## SIZE AND DEPTH (M=million)

| OCEAN | AREA | AVERAGE DEPTH |
|---|---|---|
| Pacific Ocean | 64 M sq miles (166 M sq km) | 14,042 ft (4,280 m) |
| Atlantic Ocean | 32 M sq miles (82 M sq km) | 10,827 ft (3,300 m) |
| Indian Ocean | 29 M sq miles (74 M sq km) | 12,763 ft (3,890 m) |
| Arctic Ocean | 5 M sq miles (12 M sq km) | 3,248 ft (990 m) |
| Southern Ocean | 14 M sq miles (35 M sq km) | 10,991 ft (3,350 m) |

▲ THE WATER OF LIFE
Liquid water is essential to life on Earth, and probably anywhere else in the universe. It is a vital part of the tissues of living things, and it carries the chemicals that form the complex molecules of proteins and deoxyribonucleic acid (DNA). The presence of these chemicals in seawater may have enabled life to begin in the oceans more than 3.5 billion years ago.

OFFSHORE OIL RIG ►
The oceans are rich sources of food, oil, minerals, and other natural resources, and they have been exploited as trade routes for centuries. But they are also dangerous environments with immense destructive power and are impossible to explore without special equipment. This is why the oceans are the last frontier of exploration on Earth.

# OCEAN PIONEERS

The first people to venture far from shore were not interested in the oceans themselves, but in the lands that might lie beyond them. Some of the earliest navigators were people who were seeking new places to live, like the Polynesians who were settling on many of the Pacific islands some 2,000 years ago. Later explorers were motivated by trade and plunder, but by then people were already exploring the oceans for their own sake, to map them and discover their secrets.

▲ ANCIENT MARINERS
The earliest ocean explorers may have been native Australians, who crossed the Timor Sea from Indonesia more than 50,000 years ago. About 3,500 years ago, the Polynesians set out from the western fringes of the Pacific to spread slowly across the biggest ocean on Earth. More than 1,000 years ago, the Vikings were probing west across the Atlantic in their sailing ships, as seen here in this Viking carving, reaching America 500 years before Christopher Columbus (1451–1506).

pioneers

◄ ORIENTAL FLEETS
The Chinese admiral Zheng He (1371–1433) was one of the first explorers of the Indian Ocean. He made seven voyages in the early 1400s, visiting India, Arabia, and eastern Africa. He commanded a huge fleet of more than 300 ships, including a giant nine-masted vessel that was five times the size of the ship in which Columbus crossed the Atlantic in 1492.

FERDINAND MAGELLAN ►
The first round-the-world voyage was accidental. In 1519, Ferdinand Magellan (1480–1521) headed west across the Atlantic and Pacific to reach the Indonesian Spice Islands without crossing the Indian Ocean, which was controlled by the Portuguese. He meant to come back the same way, but when he was killed in a fight his crew decided to keep sailing west, across the Indian Ocean and back into the Atlantic. Of the 265 men who set out on the voyage, just 18 returned.

► FINDING THE WAY
The early navigators did not have accurate charts or instruments. They used the position of the Sun and stars to judge how far north they were, but could only guess how far east or west they had sailed. This demanded a clock that would work accurately at sea. When such a clock was perfected by English clockmaker John Harrison (1693–1776) in the 18th century, it revolutionized sea navigation.

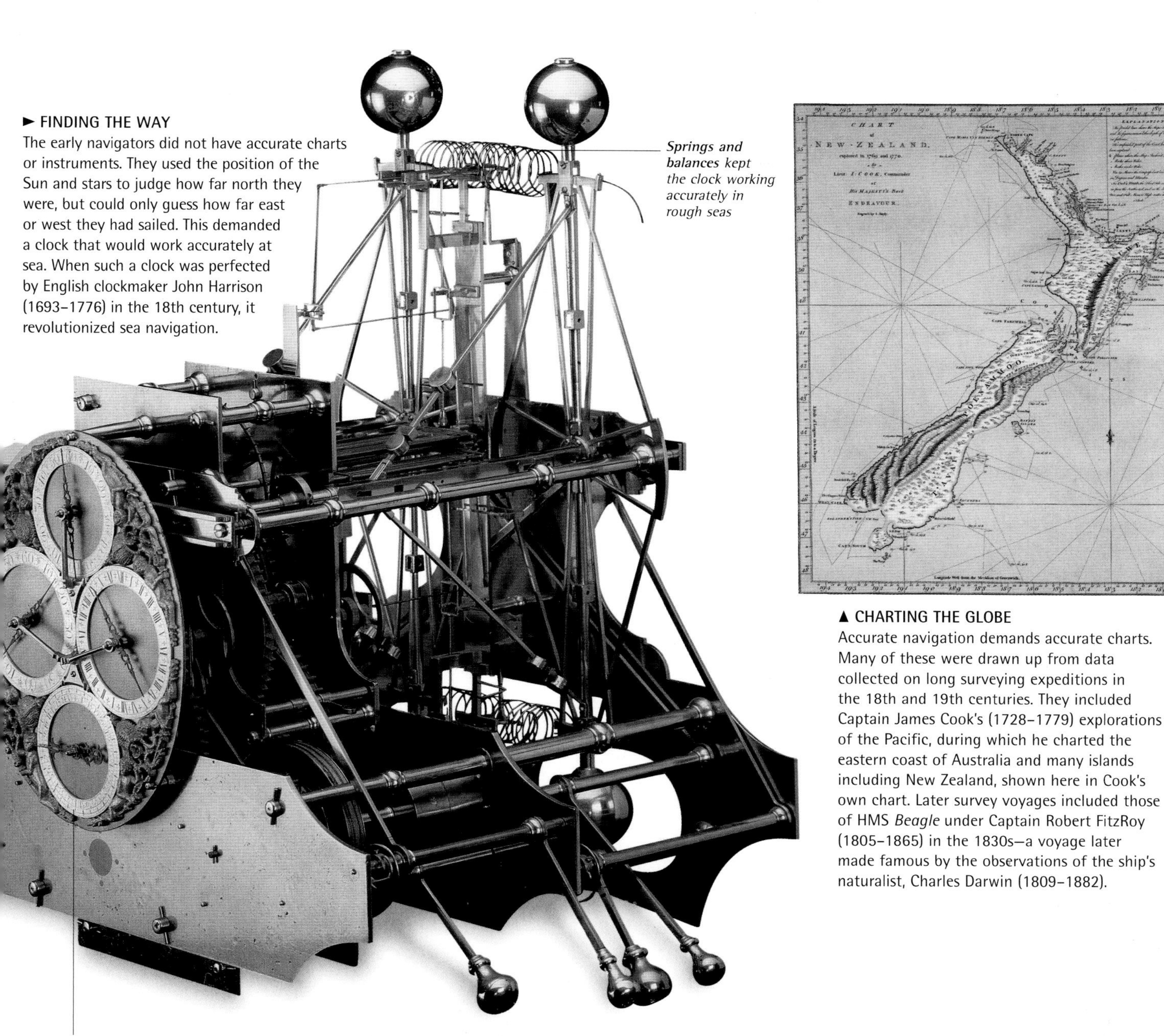

***Springs and balances** kept the clock working accurately in rough seas*

***Dials for days, hours, minutes, and seconds** were a feature of Harrison's first successful clock*

▲ CHARTING THE GLOBE
Accurate navigation demands accurate charts. Many of these were drawn up from data collected on long surveying expeditions in the 18th and 19th centuries. They included Captain James Cook's (1728–1779) explorations of the Pacific, during which he charted the eastern coast of Australia and many islands including New Zealand, shown here in Cook's own chart. Later survey voyages included those of HMS *Beagle* under Captain Robert FitzRoy (1805–1865) in the 1830s—a voyage later made famous by the observations of the ship's naturalist, Charles Darwin (1809–1882).

► THE ENDS OF THE EARTH
The last of the world's oceans to be accurately surveyed were the icy waters of the Arctic and Antarctic. Many ships and crews were lost during attempts to find a northwest passage through the Arctic Ocean to Asia. The Southern Ocean around Antarctica was even more hazardous, but was gradually charted by explorers such as Charles Wilkes (1798–1877) and James Clark Ross (1800–1862). This painting shows Ross's two ships HMS *Erebus* and HMS *Terror* in 1842, threatened by towering Antarctic icebergs.

# OCEANOGRAPHY

Oceanographic research was pioneered during the voyages of Captain James Cook (1728–1779) and Charles Darwin (1809–1882), who gathered valuable information on ocean currents, temperatures, and depths, as well as oceanic geology and marine life. But the real science of oceanography began with the voyage of HMS *Challenger* in the late 19th century. This voyage was planned with the sole object of gathering as much data about the oceans as possible. It formed the foundation of further research, all coordinated by land-based oceanographic institutions.

▲ SHIP'S NATURALIST
The main object of the 19th-century voyages was to discover and chart new lands, along with any hazards to navigation. But they also carried scientists on board—most famously Charles Darwin, who joined the 1831–36 voyage of HMS *Beagle*, shown here anchored off Tierra del Fuego. While at sea, Darwin collected marine organisms, examined the nature of ocean water, and speculated on the origins of volcanic islands, coral reefs, and atolls, and the species that lived on them.

▲ THE CHALLENGER EXPEDITION
The 1872–76 voyage of HMS *Challenger*—an ex-survey ship—was the first attempt to understand how oceans work. The physicists, chemists, and biologists on board measured and sampled everything possible by dredging, trawling, and taking soundings using long cables—even in the deepest parts of the ocean. In the process they discovered more than 4,700 new species and gained a rough picture of the ocean floor with its ridges, chasms, and abyssal plains.

▲ MODERN OCEANOGRAPHIC RESEARCH
Modern research ships gather data on oceans throughout the world, feeding it back to oceanographic institutes such as Woods Hole and Scripps in the US, and at Southampton and Naples in Europe. These institutions draw together the many sciences involved in oceanography, including oceanic physics and chemistry, marine biology, geology, and meteorology. The complex interaction of all these disciplines makes oceanography one of the most demanding sciences.

► SONAR SURVEYS
The early research ships spent a lot of time measuring ocean depths using extremely long, weighted sounding lines. This gave way to echo-sounding or sonar techniques, and eventually side-scan sonar, which produces 3-D views, as in this image of the Pacific ocean floor off South America.

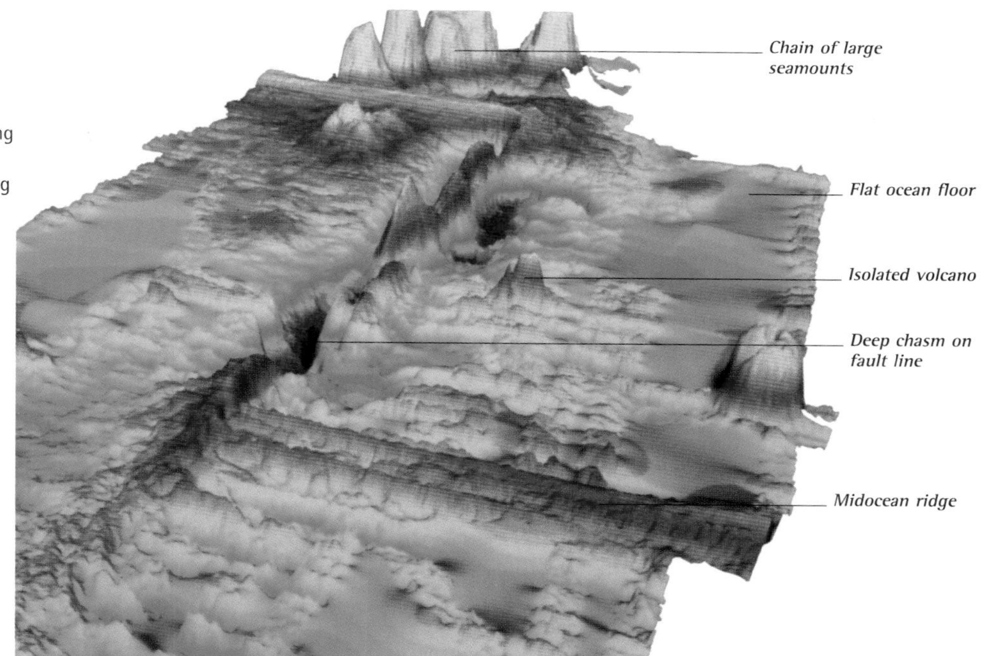


◄ DEEP-SEA DRILLING
Many oceanic theories have been investigated by sampling the rocks of the ocean floor at various places and depths to build up a picture of its composition. The Japanese drilling vessel *Chikyu* can drill to depths of 23,000 ft (7,000 m) or more below the ocean floor, in waters 8,200 ft (2,500 m) deep—a total depth greater than the height of Mount Everest.

SATELLITE INFORMATION

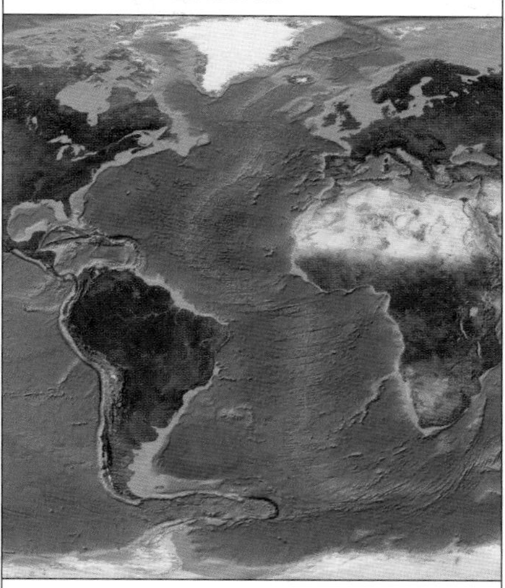

Data collected by satellites has proved extremely valuable to oceanographers. Gravity measurements taken by sensors mounted on satellites have provided the most accurate images yet of the ocean floors, as in this image of the Atlantic Ocean. Other sensors are able to gather data on temperatures, ice cover, ocean currents, and plankton distribution, which can then be used to build up accurate, up-to-date maps. Satellite images also give us superb views of oceanic weather systems, including hurricanes.

# EXPLORING THE OCEAN DEPTHS

For centuries, people have been exploring shallow seas using simple diving bells. However, the crushing pressures at greater depths made deep-ocean exploration impossible, until the development of deep-water submersibles. The first of these were little more than pressure-proof metal spheres, equipped with weights and floats for sinking and rising. *Alvin*, built in 1962, was the first of a new generation of manned craft that could be easily maneuvered underwater to gather samples and record images of the deep ocean floor.

◄ DIVING BELL
Diving bells were being used for salvaging wrecks as early as 1690. These were often built of wood, made watertight above, but with an opening at the bottom, and suspended from a mother ship by a cable. As the bell was lowered to the seabed, air pressure inside it stopped the water level from rising inside. A diver could also work on the seabed wearing a helmet to which air was piped from the diving bell.

◄ ALVIN
Owned by the US Navy, but operated by the Woods Hole Oceanographic Institution in New England, *Alvin* can carry two scientists and a pilot to a maximum depth of 15,000 ft (4,500 m). Since its first dive in 1964, it has made more than 4,000 descents, discovering deep-sea hydrothermal vents in 1977 and making the first manned survey of the *Titanic*.

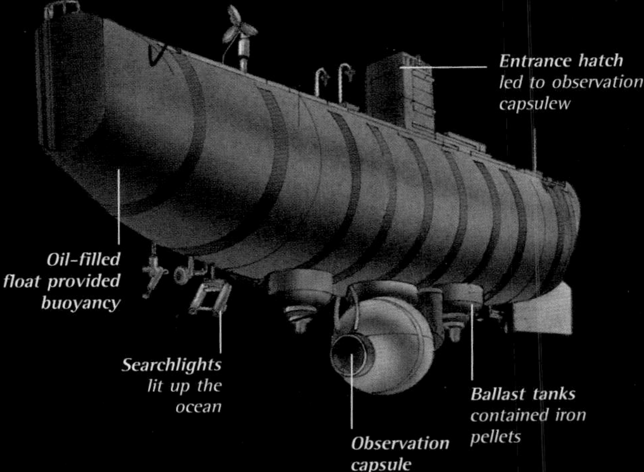


▲ THE BATHYSCAPHE
In 1960, Jacques Piccard (born 1922) and Don Walsh (born 1931) descended into the deepest part of the Pacific in the bathyscaphe *Trieste*. This was basically a metal sphere suspended from a huge oil-filled float, and weighed down with iron ballast. After sinking for several hours, they spent 20 minutes on the ocean floor before releasing the ballast to return to the surface. But they saw a fish there, proving that life exists in extreme depths.

◄ MANNED SUBMERSIBLES
At a depth of about 13,000 ft (4,000 m), a dive to the ocean floor takes at least two hours, with the scientists and pilot crammed into a small and uncomfortable but very strong metal sphere. They leave the outside lights off to save power, but switch them on when they reach the bottom so that they can see, explore, gather samples, and send video images back to the mother ship.

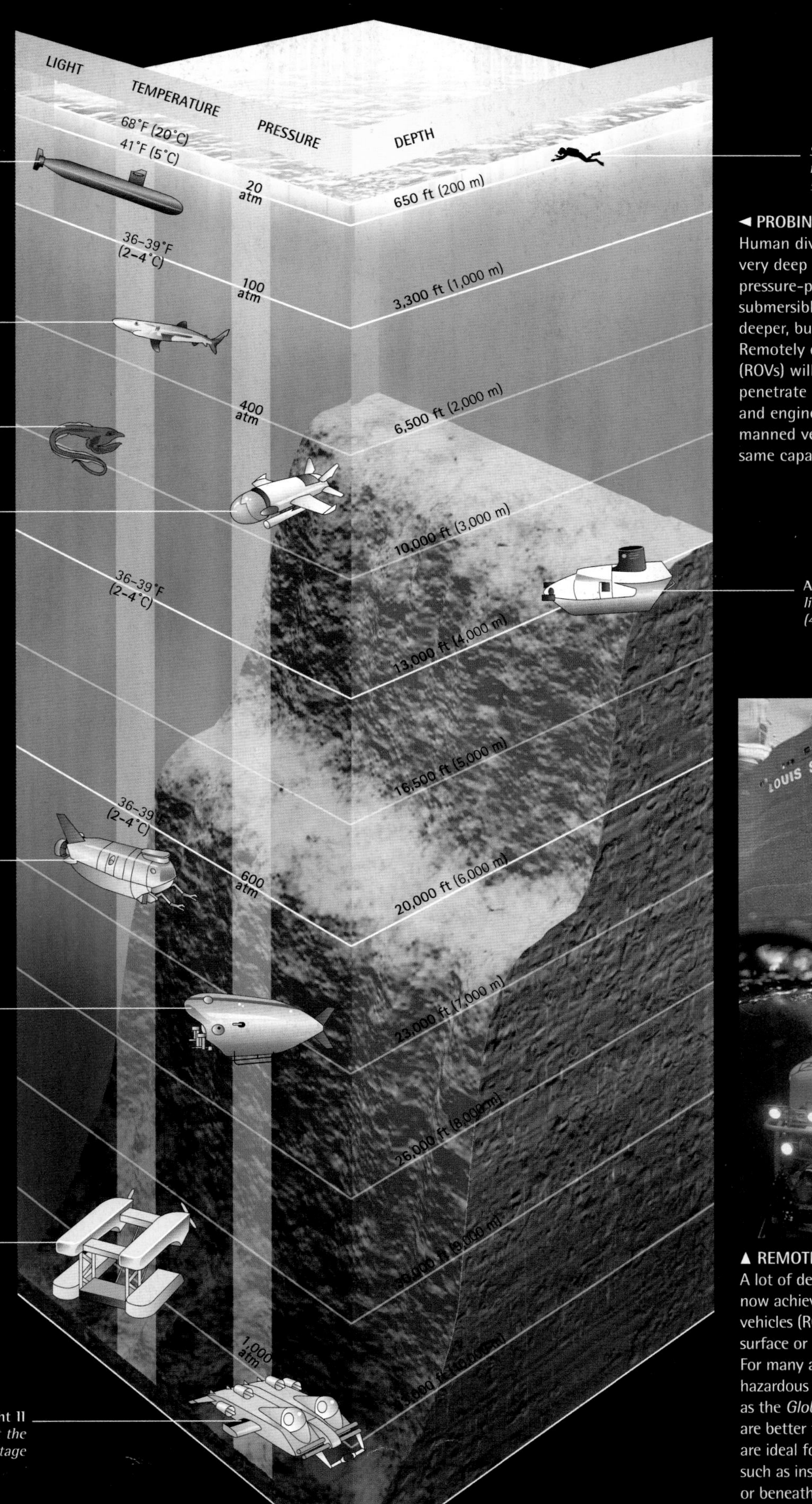


***Nuclear submarine*** *cannot withstand the pressures in the deep ocean*

***Great white shark*** *can dive much deeper than a submarine*

***Gulper eel,*** *like many other fish, is not affected by intense pressure*

**Deep Flight I** *uses aircraft technology to "fly" underwater*

**ocean depths**

**Shinkai 6500** *has dived to 21,447 ft (6,537 m)*

***COMRA vehicle*** *is designed to reach 23,000 ft (7,000 m)*

***This Hybrid ROV*** *will operate at extreme depths*

**Deep Flight II** *is still at the design stage*

***Scuba diver*** *at a maximum depth of 50 m* ***(164 ft)***

**Alvin** *has a depth limit of 14,746 ft (4,500 m)*

**◄ PROBING THE DEEP**

Human divers cannot dive very deep without special pressure-proof suits. Pressurized submersibles can venture much deeper, but each has its limits. Remotely operated vehicles (ROVs) will soon be able to penetrate deep ocean trenches, and engineers are working on manned vehicles with the same capabilities.

**▲ REMOTE CONTROL**

A lot of deep-ocean exploration is now achieved using remotely operated vehicles (ROVs), with video links to the surface or to manned submersibles. For many applications—especially hazardous situations—ROVs such as the *Global Explorer* (shown above) are better than manned craft. They are ideal for investigating cavities such as inside wrecks and caves, or beneath the polar ice.

# THE OCEAN FLOORS

Since the ocean depths were first investigated in the 19th century, scientists have known that they are not just featureless basins filled with water. They found that oceans are fringed by shallow coastal seas, and that the deeper regions are dotted with submarine volcanoes and long mountain ridges. They also discovered trenches that plunge to extraordinary depths in the ocean floors. The data collected enabled them to produce amazing maps showing these features in graphic detail.

*Abyssal plain* *covered by sediment*

*Seamount* *or submerged mountain*

*Midoceanic ridge* *of underwater mountains*

*Trench* *in ocean floor*

*Volcanic islands* *forming chain near trench*

*Shallow coastal sea* *on ocean fringe*

▲ OCEAN TOPOGRAPHY
A section across an ocean floor shows that it has a much greater range of topography than a typical continent. Oceans have long midocean ridges cut by vast fault lines. They are peppered with islands and submerged mountains, sometimes forming long chains. The fringes of most of the Pacific and northeast Indian Ocean are marked by deep trenches, some of which are three times the average depth of the world's oceans.

## OCEAN FLOOR FEATURES

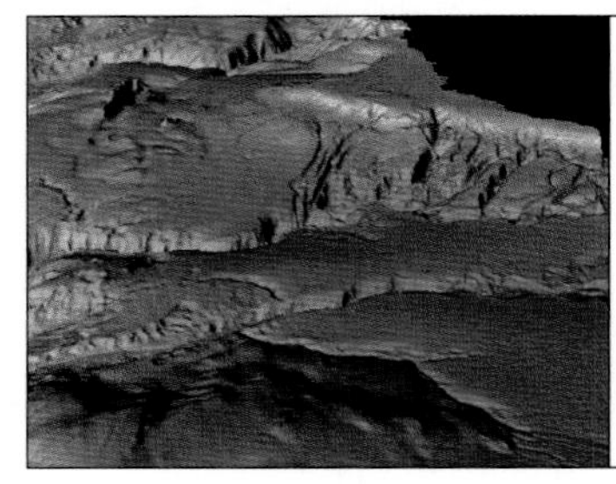

CONTINENTAL SHELVES
The shallow regions at the fringes of oceans are the continental shelves. They can extend a long way from the coast, seen here in black, and are often cut by deep canyons. At their outer edges, the continental shelves slope down to the ocean floor.

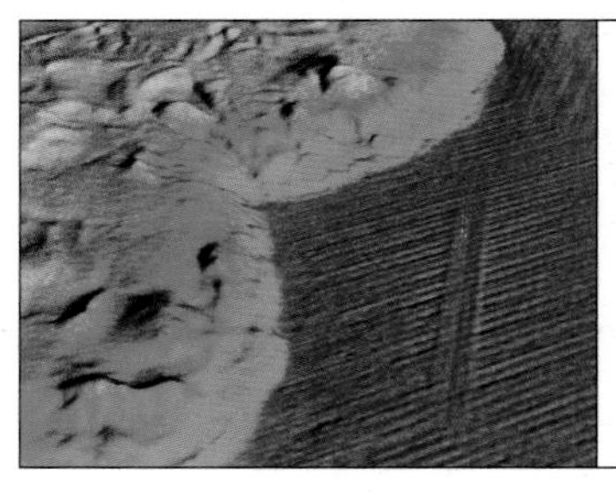

ABYSSAL PLAINS
Great tracts of ocean floor are covered with soft mud, sand, and other sediments. These form the abyssal plains, seen here in blue. The layers of sediments are often very deep, masking the rugged contours of the oceanic bedrock below.

MIDOCEAN RIDGES
Shown in red is an isolated seamount and part of a midocean ridge. These ridges are the longest mountain chains on Earth, and they join up to form a network around the globe. They all form rugged peaks of dark basalt rock.

OCEAN TRENCHES
A satellite image shows an ocean trench in dark blue, lying between the deep ocean and the shallow seas off Asia. Linked with earthquakes and volcanoes, some of these trenches are deep enough to swallow the highest mountains on Earth.

► EXAGGERATED HEIGHTS AND SLOPES
On all maps and illustrations of the ocean floor, vertical distances are hugely exaggerated so that the features are easy to see. Undersea volcanoes and islands seem to rise from the ocean floor like needles, while trenches and shelves look like canyons and cliffs. In reality, these features are far less dramatic.

*Volcanic island* *is shown far too high*

AN OCEAN FLOOR MAP ▲
The development of echo-sounding in the 1920s enabled ships to record ocean depths easily and quickly. As the data built up, it started to create a picture of the ocean floors. This was made a reality in the 1970s, with the publication of the first world ocean floor map by American marine geologist Bruce Heezen (1924–1977) and his research assistant Marie Tharp (1920–2006), seen above. The map (right) was put together using simple depth figures, so a lot of the detail was based on educated guesswork. But it was a vivid representation of the ocean floors, and the patterns and features that it revealed inspired both its makers and other scientists to discover more about how the oceans were formed.

▼ MORE REALISTIC HEIGHTS AND SLOPES
In reality, oceanic volcanoes are broad domes, and the gradients at the edges of shallow coastal seas are so shallow that, if these gradients were on land, you could ride a bicycle up them. Even deep ocean trenches are broad troughs rather than steep-sided chasms. This illustration shows a more realistic view of the scene depicted opposite.

***Volcanic island*** *as it is in reality*

# OCEANS AND CONTINENTS

Ocean basins are not just water-filled hollows in the Earth's surface. They are quite different from the continents that divide them. The heavy bedrock of ocean floors is the thin crust of the hot mantle that forms most of the planet, while continents are made of thicker slabs of lighter rock that float on the mantle like rafts. The continents are dragged slowly around the world by currents within the mantle. Oceans form where continents are pulled apart, and are destroyed where continents are pushed together.

*Upper mantle:* *partly molten rock, 416 miles (670 km) thick; temperature 1,800°F (1,000°C)*

*Inner core:* *solid metals about 1,500 miles (2,440 km) across; temperature 12,600°F (7,000°C)*

*Outer core:* *liquid metals about 1,400 miles (2,250 km) thick; temperature 7,200°F (4,000°C)*

*Lower mantle:* *solid rock, 1,400 miles (2,230 km) thick; temperature 6,300°F (3,500°C)*

THE LAYERED EARTH ►
The Earth was formed from asteroids that were drawn together by gravity to form a rocky sphere. As they collided they released enough energy to melt the entire planet. Most of the heavy metal in the rock sank to the center to form its metallic core. The rock around the core became the solid but very hot mantle, and the skin of the mantle cooled to form the Earth's crust.

*Continental shelf*

*Continental crust*

*Oceanic crust*

*Upper mantle*

*Lower mantle*

◄ THE EARTH'S CRUST
The heavy, dark rock of the oceanic crust is similar to the rock of the upper mantle, and is just 4–7 miles (6–11 km) thick. By contrast, the continental crust is up to 55 miles (90 km) thick, but its rocks weigh less than the rocks that form the ocean floor. The continental shelves are the submerged edges of the continents, drowned by shallow coastal seas.

## MANTLE AND CRUST ROCKS

PERIDOTITE
The upper mantle is made of peridotite, a very heavy rock that contains a lot of iron and another metal, magnesium. Peridotite occurs in just a few places where it has been squeezed up from beneath the ocean floor.

BASALT
Oceanic crust is made of basalt. This is basically peridotite that has lost some of its heavier ingredients. Basalt erupts from oceanic volcanoes as very liquid lava, which cools to form a black rock that gradually turns rusty brown on the outside.

GRANITE
Continental crust is made up of many rocks, but one of the most common is granite. It is formed from molten rock that has cooled very slowly, deep in the ground. Granite has a lower metal content than basalt, so it is lighter. This is why it "floats" on the dense, heavy mantle.

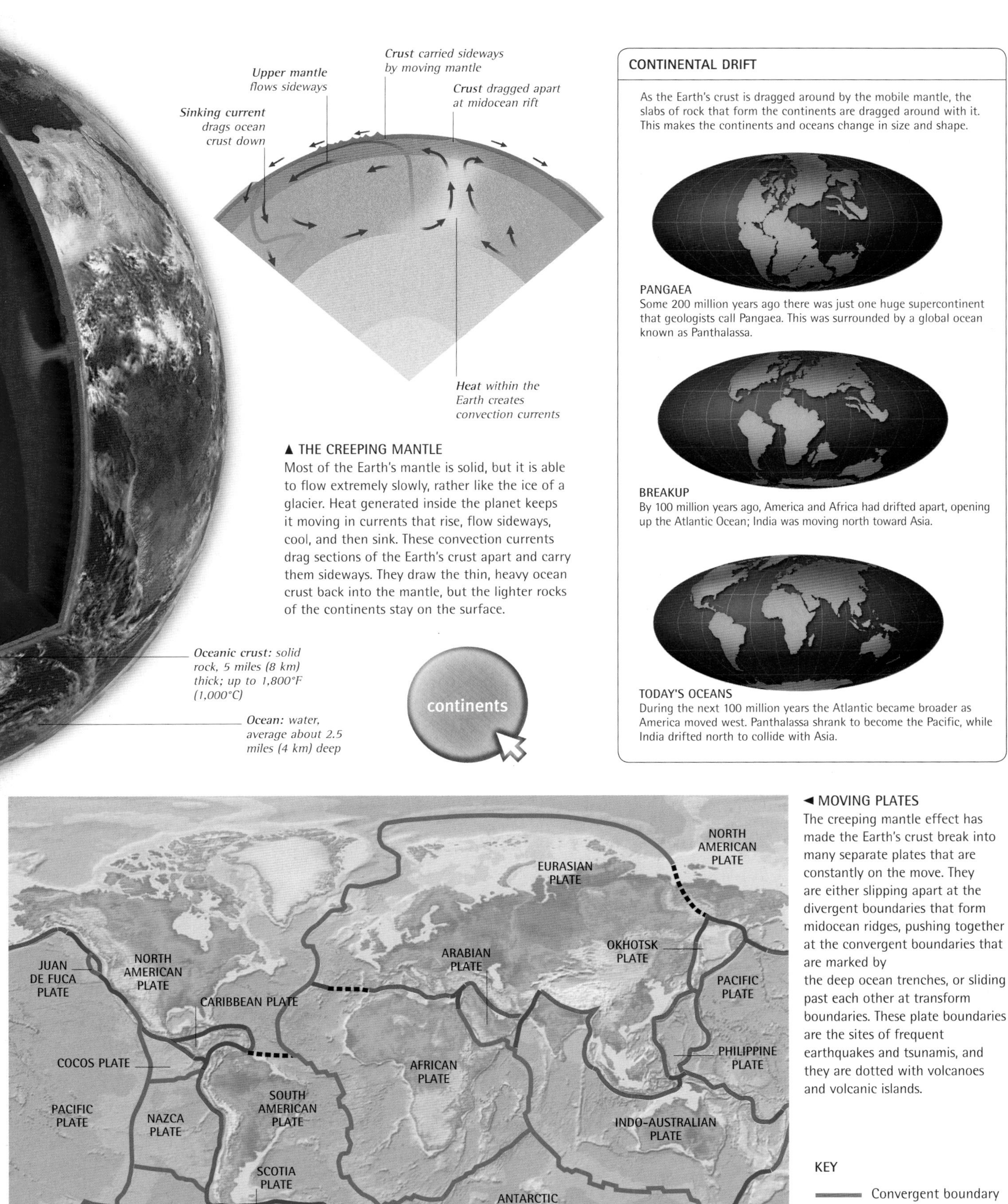


▲ THE CREEPING MANTLE

Most of the Earth's mantle is solid, but it is able to flow extremely slowly, rather like the ice of a glacier. Heat generated inside the planet keeps it moving in currents that rise, flow sideways, cool, and then sink. These convection currents drag sections of the Earth's crust apart and carry them sideways. They draw the thin, heavy ocean crust back into the mantle, but the lighter rocks of the continents stay on the surface.

## CONTINENTAL DRIFT

As the Earth's crust is dragged around by the mobile mantle, the slabs of rock that form the continents are dragged around with it. This makes the continents and oceans change in size and shape.

PANGAEA

Some 200 million years ago there was just one huge supercontinent that geologists call Pangaea. This was surrounded by a global ocean known as Panthalassa.

BREAKUP

By 100 million years ago, America and Africa had drifted apart, opening up the Atlantic Ocean; India was moving north toward Asia.

TODAY'S OCEANS

During the next 100 million years the Atlantic became broader as America moved west. Panthalassa shrank to become the Pacific, while India drifted north to collide with Asia.

◄ MOVING PLATES

The creeping mantle effect has made the Earth's crust break into many separate plates that are constantly on the move. They are either slipping apart at the divergent boundaries that form midocean ridges, pushing together at the convergent boundaries that are marked by the deep ocean trenches, or sliding past each other at transform boundaries. These plate boundaries are the sites of frequent earthquakes and tsunamis, and they are dotted with volcanoes and volcanic islands.

KEY

- Convergent boundary
- Divergent boundary
- Transform boundary
- Uncertain boundary

# MIDOCEAN RIDGES

Ocean floor is formed where plates of oceanic crust move apart to create a spreading rift. This relieves pressure on the hot mantle rock below, and since pressure is all that keeps the hot rock solid, it turns into molten magma and squirts up through the rift as basalt lava. The lava cools in the cold ocean waters to form the solid rock of the ocean floor. Meanwhile, the magma chamber beneath the rift makes the rock expand, raising the crust on each side of the rift into two lines of submarine mountains that form a midocean ridge.

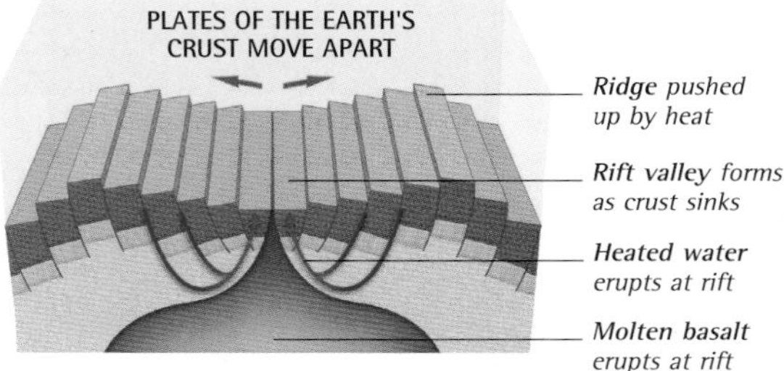


▲ SPREADING RIFT
Where the ocean floor is being pulled apart by convection currents in the hot mantle below, big blocks of oceanic crust sink to form a rift valley at the boundary. The floor of the valley is full of fissures, which erupt basalt lava and superheated water rich in dissolved chemicals. On each side of the rift, blocks of ocean crust are raised into ridges by the heat, but they gradually sink again as they slowly move away from the hot zone.

◄ WINDING RIDGES
The midocean ridges created by rifting and uplift extend for vast distances across the ocean floor. The Mid-Atlantic Ridge—seen here on the Heezen-Tharp map—extends for about 10,000 miles (16,000 km), all the way from the Southern Ocean to the Arctic Ocean. Its mountains are up to 13,000 ft (4,000 m) high, but their peaks lie 6,500 ft (2,000 m) beneath the surface of the ocean.

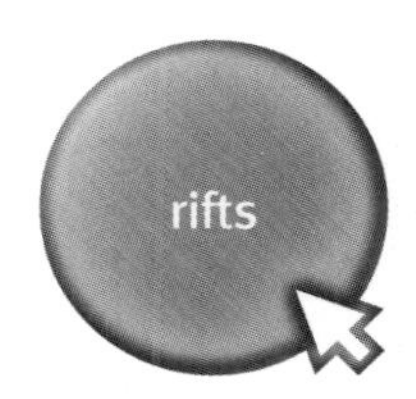


*Earthquake zone*
*Transform fault*
*Rift offset by transform fault*
*Magma rising beneath spreading rift*
*Movement of oceanic plate*

◄ TRANSFORM FAULTS
Midocean ridges are split into short sections divided by long transform faults that cut straight across them. These faults are very obvious features of the ocean floor map shown on the far left. They are caused by slightly different spreading rates along the rift. Where they link sections of the spreading rift, the ocean floor on either side of the fault is moving in opposite directions, and this causes submarine earthquakes.

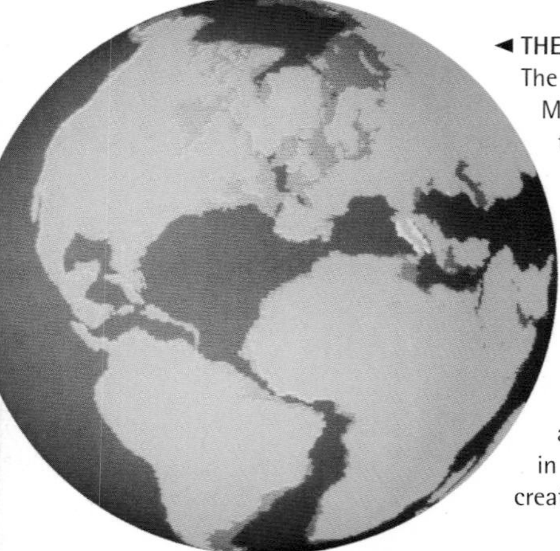

◄ THE OPENING ATLANTIC
The winding route of the Mid-Atlantic Ridge echoes the shapes of South America and Africa. This is not a coincidence. Some 130 million years ago the two continents were joined together, but then a rift opened up between them, as seen here. The rift was flooded with water, and a new ocean floor formed in the widening gap to create the Atlantic Ocean.

▲ BILLOWING LAVA
Basalt lava squirts up through fissures in the spreading rift at temperatures of about 1,800°F (1,000°C), but then hits deep-ocean water that is close to freezing point. The lava hardens instantly on the outside, but then bursts out through the hardened shell to form a series of rounded lobes. When these finally become solid they look like black cushions, so they are called pillow lavas. In a few places, where the Earth's crust has been uplifted, these can be seen on land.

BLACK SMOKERS ►
Ocean water that seeps into deep fissures in the rift zone is heated by contact with hot rock. But the high pressure at these depths stops it from boiling and turning to water vapor at the usual 212°F (100°C), and it is often superheated to 752°F (400°C) or more before it erupts from the ocean floor. Dissolved chemicals may turn the water black as it erupts, and so these hydrothermal vents are also known as black smokers.

*Heated chemicals form sootlike particles when they mix with cold water*

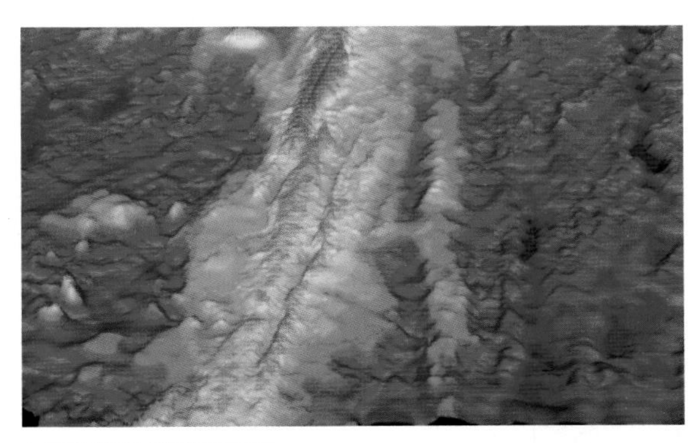

▲ THE EAST PACIFIC RISE
The Mid-Atlantic Ridge is spreading at about 2 in (4 cm) a year, but other midocean ridges are spreading faster. The East Pacific Rise to the south of Mexico, seen here in a sonar image, is spreading at 9 in (22 cm) a year. Yet, although it is more active, its submarine mountains are not so high, because the hotter, softer rock beneath the ridge cannot support big, heavy peaks. The rift is peppered with underwater volcanoes and clusters of hydrothermal vents.

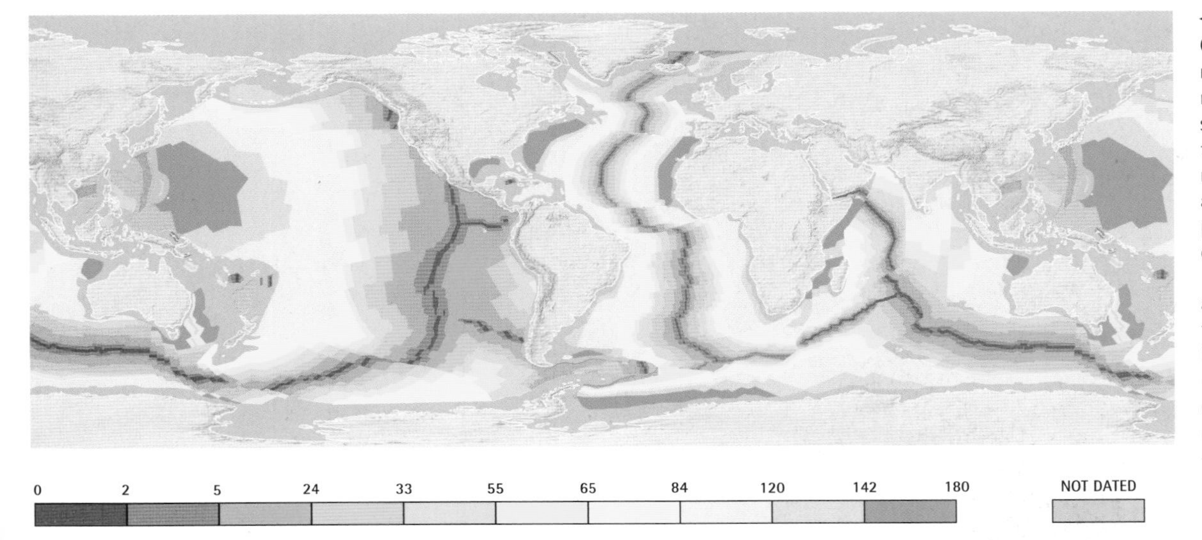


◄ OCEAN FLOOR AGE
Ocean floor is formed at midocean ridges, and gradually moves away from them on both sides as more rock erupts from the spreading rifts. So the rocks near the ridges are the youngest, and those farther away get progressively older. But no part of the ocean floor is more than 180 million years old, because any oceanic rocks formed before this time have been drawn back into the mantle and recycled. By comparison, the oldest continental rocks are 3,800 million years old. The map and key show the ocean floor age in millions of years.

# HOTSPOTS AND SEAMOUNTS

Not all oceanic crust is formed at the spreading rifts of midocean ridges. The hot mantle of the Earth is dotted with extra-hot regions known as mantle plumes. Many of these lie well away from the boundaries between the plates of the Earth's crust. They form stationary hotspots that burn through the crust, erupting molten lava that builds up into volcanoes. As each volcano is carried away from the hotspot by the moving crust it becomes extinct, and another volcano erupts over the hotspot. This process has created chains of volcanic islands and thousands of submerged volcanoes known as seamounts.

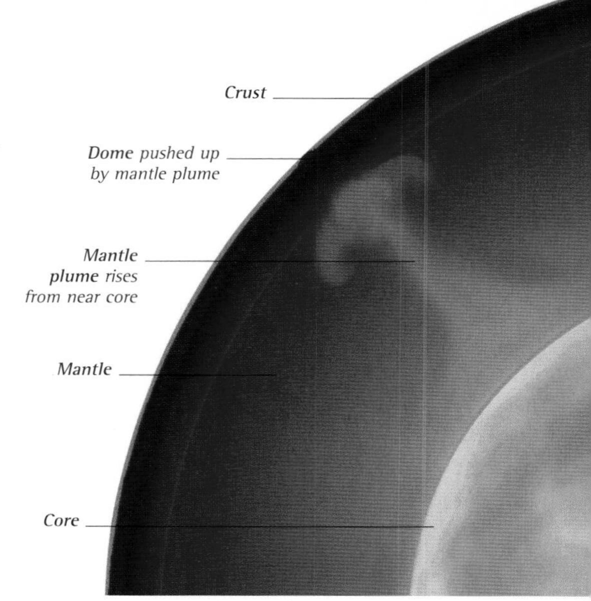


▲ MANTLE PLUMES
The mantle plumes that cause hotspots probably rise from deep in the mantle near the Earth's core. Each plume pushes up a broad dome in the oceanic crust— 600 miles (1,000 km) across and 1 mile (1.6 km) high in the case of Hawaii—and an even higher volcano erupts from the center of the dome.

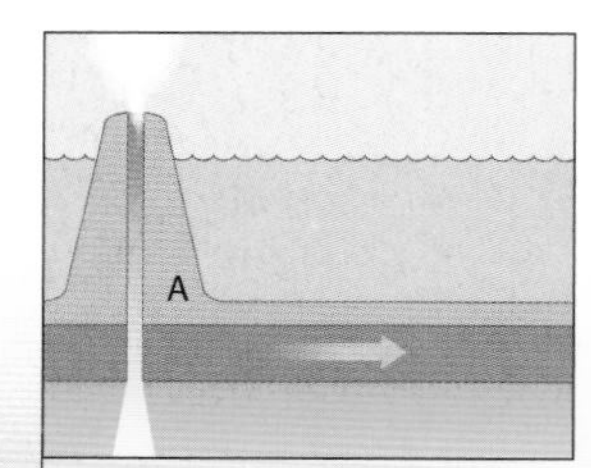


1 *First volcano erupts over hotspot to create an island*

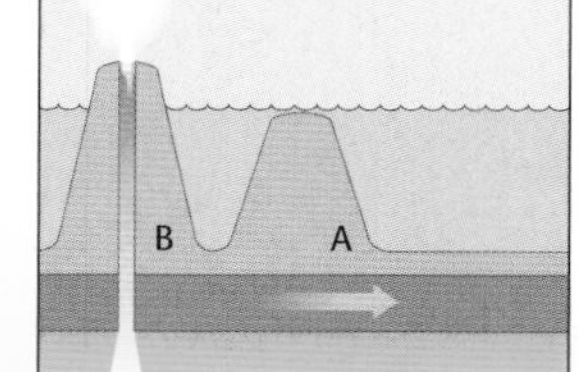


2 *Volcano drifts off hotspot and becomes extinct while a new one erupts*

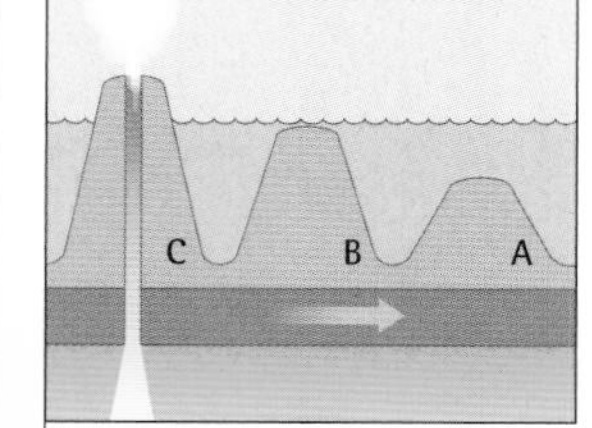


3 *Extinct volcanoes slowly sink as another volcano erupts*

◄ VOLCANIC CHAINS
The hotspot burns a hole through the Earth's crust, creating a volcano (A). But the mobile crust carries the volcano away from the hotspot, so it becomes extinct and starts sinking. A new one erupts (B), but that is also slowly carried off the hotspot, too. By the time a third volcano appears (C), the oldest may have sunk below the waves.

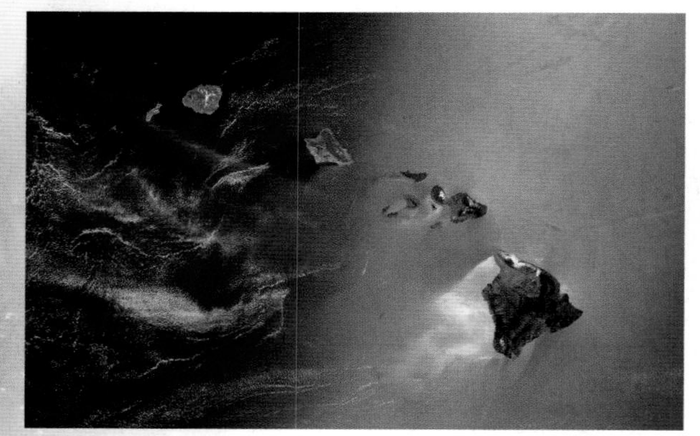

▲ HAWAII
The islands of Hawaii, seen here from space, have been created by the Pacific Ocean plate slipping northwest over a hotspot at about 3 in (9 cm) a year. The hotspot is currently beneath the highly active volcano on the biggest southeastern island. Meanwhile, the extinct volcanoes to the north are slowly sinking, and will become progressively smaller until they dwindle to a long chain of submerged seamounts.

◄ FIRE FOUNTAINS
The volcanoes of Hawaii are huge domes that rise from the ocean floor. The largest, Mauna Loa, is higher from base to summit than Mount Everest in the Himalayas. Kilauea, on the flanks of Mauna Loa, is the most active volcano on Earth, constantly erupting fire fountains of fluid basalt lava that flow down to the sea in rivers of molten rock.

▲ FIRE AND ICE
The volcanic island of Iceland has been created by a vast outpouring of basalt lava, from a hotspot under the northern end of the Mid-Atlantic Ridge. Iceland has many active volcanoes, including one that lies beneath a sheet of ice, and water seeping down into the hot rock beneath the island erupts in geysers of superheated water and steam.

## OTHER HOTSPOT ISLANDS

GALÁPAGOS
These volcanic islands formed on a plate moving east over a Pacific hotspot. The islands carried farther to the east are the oldest, while those in the west are still volcanically active. They are famous for their unique wildlife, like these marine iguanas.

EASTER ISLAND
The famous Easter Island statues are carved from volcanic ash erupted by three volcanoes formed over a Pacific hotspot about 3 million years ago. The triangular island they created has since drifted off the hotspot, and the volcanoes are now extinct.

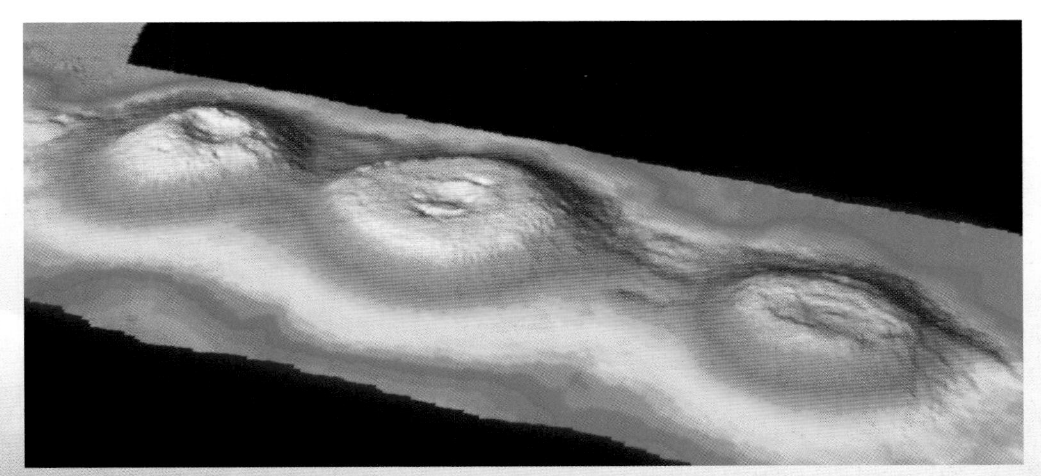

SEAMOUNTS AND GUYOTS ►
Most volcanoes that erupt from the ocean floor never reach the surface, as seen here in a sonar image. Some of these seamounts were volcanic islands, but have sunk again. Worn flat on top by waves, they are called guyots after their discoverer, Henry Guyot (1807–1884).

► OCEAN RIDGES
Volcanic activity on the ocean floors has also created many long ridges of seamounts that have become joined together, especially in the Indian Ocean. These form the foundation for coral islands like the Maldives.

# OCEAN TRENCHES

As new sections of ocean floor are formed at midocean ridges, some oceans like the Atlantic grow wider each year. But the planet is not getting any bigger. While some ocean floors expand, others shrink. Their edges sink back into the hot mantle along destructive plate margins known as subduction zones. The process creates deep ocean trenches and long lines of volcanoes, pushes up mountain ranges, and causes earthquakes and tsunamis.

*Ocean floor carried east by currents in the mantle*

*Oceanic crust dragged under lighter continent*

▲ DESTRUCTIVE MARGINS
Oceanic crust that is formed at a midocean ridge gradually spreads away from the ridge, driven by currents in the mantle below. This may simply make the ocean wider, but in the eastern Pacific, for example, oceanic crust moves east until it reaches the Peru–Chile Trench off South America. Here, it is dragged beneath the lighter crust of the continent and eventually destroyed.

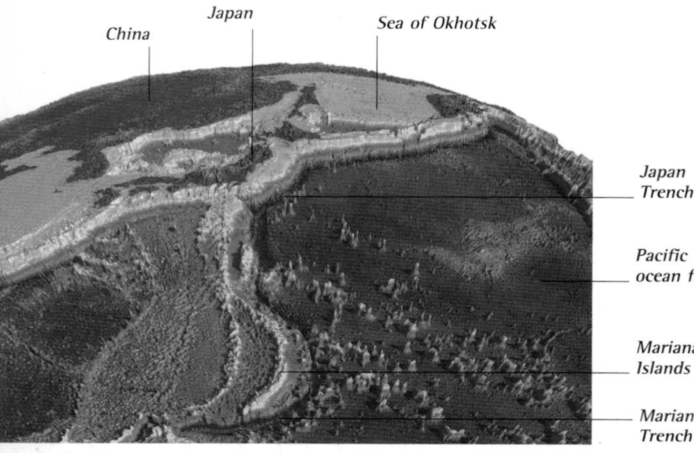


◄ SUBMARINE CHASMS
The subduction zones where the crust is destroyed are marked by deep ocean trenches, often associated with chains of volcanic islands. These trenches have been created by the ocean floor being dragged down into the hot heart of the planet by descending currents in the mantle. Although they are partly or even completely filled with sediments, some can be three times as deep as the nearby ocean floor. The lowest point of the Mariana Trench in the western Pacific lies nearly 7 miles (11 km) below the ocean surface, making it the deepest chasm on Earth.

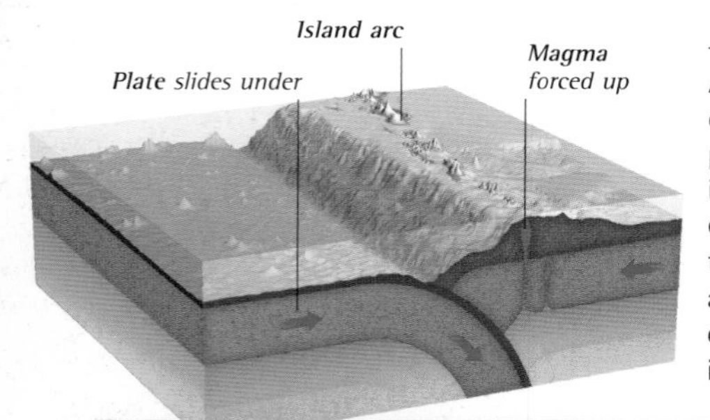


◄ OCEANIC BOUNDARY
As a subducted plate of oceanic crust plunges beneath another plate and into the hot mantle, it melts. The molten magma erupts through volcanoes in the overlying plate margin, and these often form long, curved chains of volcanic islands called island arcs.

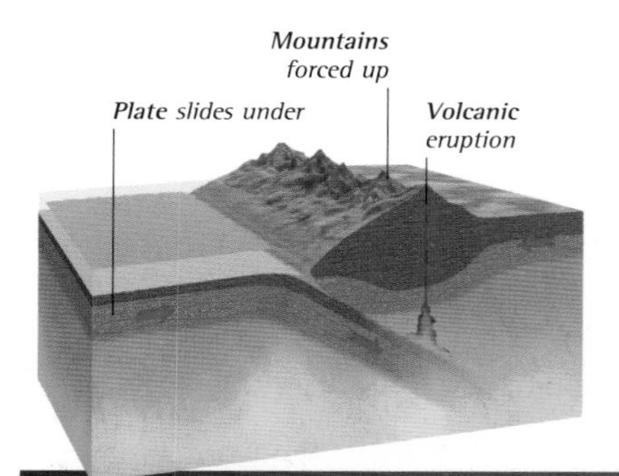


◄ CONTINENTAL BOUNDARY
Where the ocean floor is being dragged beneath a continent, such as South America, the friction buckles the continental fringe into high mountains like the Andes. The volcanoes that would form island arcs at an oceanic boundary erupt through these mountains.

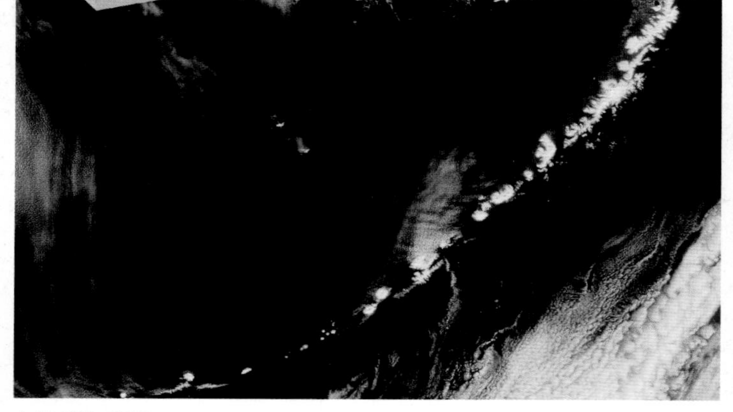

▲ ISLAND ARCS
Volcanic island arcs trace the plate margin in a curved chain like the Aleutian island arc in the north Pacific, seen here from space. Over time, the islands get bigger and join together, to form elongated islands like Java on the Sunda Arc.

▲ MOUNTAIN RANGES
The fold mountains thrown up along continental boundaries are initially high and rugged, like the Andes seen here. They are dotted with volcanoes, and the rocks often contain rare, valuable deposits such as copper, silver, and emeralds.

◄ EARTHQUAKE ZONES
The subduction zones are notorious for their earthquakes, caused by the sudden fracture of the rocks along the mobile plate boundary. The islands of Japan lie in one of these regions, along a boundary marked by the deep Japan Trench. Here, earthquakes are a daily event, with about a thousand tremors each year. Every few years a really big earthquake causes destruction on a massive scale, as in the Kobe earthquake in 1995.

## PACIFIC RING OF FIRE

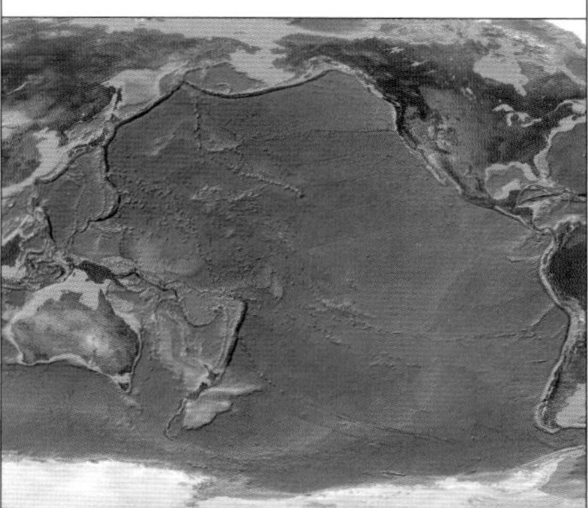

The Pacific is surrounded by ocean trenches, shown on this satellite image as dark lines extending from New Zealand to South America, and hundreds of volcanoes known as the Pacific Ring of Fire. Steady destruction of the ocean floor in such zones is shrinking the Pacific by 1 sq mile (2.5 sq km) a year.

*Volcanic rock is fragmented into ash by the force of the explosion*

▲ VOLCANIC CATACLYSMS
The lava produced by volcanoes in the subduction zones is much stickier than the lava erupted at midocean ridges. It can block the vent, building up pressure and causing explosive eruptions like that of Mount Pinatubo in the Philippines in 1991.

# TSUNAMIS

When an earthquake occurs on the ocean floor, it creates fast-moving shock waves called tsunamis. On the open ocean the waves are broad and low, with a very long wavelength from crest to crest. When they reach shallower water the waves get shorter and steeper, piling up into very high crests and equally deep troughs. Eventually, a trough reaches the coast, causing the sea to draw back by many yards. Then the wave crest strikes, often with devastating power.

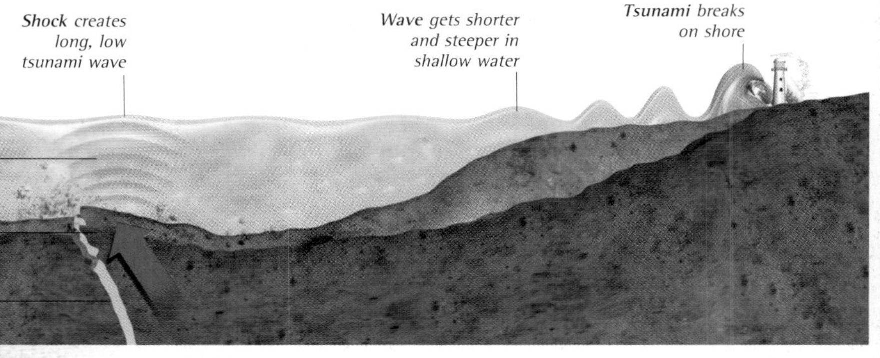


▲ SHOCK WAVE
Many earthquakes are caused by sections of the Earth's crust slipping suddenly along plate margins. In subduction zones, the steady movement of the sinking plate can drag the edge of the other plate down and then suddenly release it. The plate springs up, carrying the water up with it, which then flows out sideways as a tsunami.

◄ STRAIN AND SNAP
The plates of the Earth's crust are always moving. If they slip steadily, the movement causes small, regular tremors. But if the plates become locked against each other, the strain builds until something snaps. If the crust has distorted by 10 ft (3 m) by the time this happens, the rocks move this distance in a few seconds to release the tension. The colossal shock of this movement causes an earthquake.

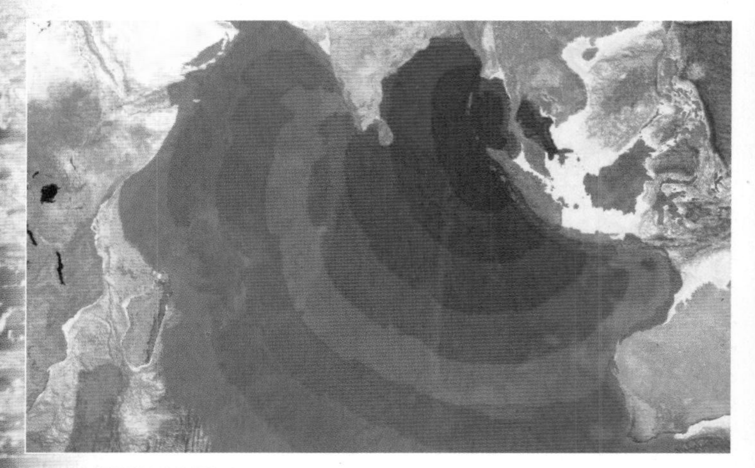

▲ RADIATING WAVES
The 2004 Asian tsunami was caused by an earthquake in the Java Trench off northern Sumatra. The rupture was 750 miles (1,200 km) long, and the rocks moved vertically by 50 ft (15 m). The resulting tsunami radiated outward across the Indian Ocean at 500 miles (800 km) per hour. Each band shows the distance traveled in one hour.

▲ CATASTROPHE
When tsunami waves reach the shore they can build up into huge mounds of water that sweep away everything in their path. This happened during the 2004 Asian tsunami when large areas of nearby Sumatra were devastated, and more than 100,000 people died in Indonesia alone. The waves had their greatest impact on human settlements, while natural habitats were less affected.

tsunamis

▲ RAISING WRECKS
The uplift of the sea floor that causes a tsunami can have dramatic effects on the nearby coastline. During the 1964 Alaskan earthquake, the Pacific floor slid 65 ft (20 m) beneath Alaska in three minutes, and raised parts of the shore by 30 ft (10 m). In the process, it lifted an offshore reef above the water, bringing with it an old shipwreck that had previously been half submerged.

▲ EARLY WARNING
After a tsunami hit Hawaii in 1946, an early warning system was set up in the Pacific to warn of similar disasters. It uses buoys to detect waves while they are still traveling across the open ocean and transmit the data to shore before a tsunami strikes. Unfortunately, there was no such system operating in the Indian Ocean in 2004.

# COASTAL EROSION

Smashing against the edges of continents, waves slowly wear away their fringes, cutting them back to form coasts but leaving the continental shelves below sea level. The rocks of exposed shores are eroded to create caves, cliffs, and rocky reefs. The debris is swept along the coast to more sheltered places where it is dumped as shingle banks, sandy beaches, and mudflats. So in some places the coast is cut back by erosion, and in others it is extended by banks and beaches.

▲ CLIFFS
Where the land surface is well above the sea level, its fringes get eroded to create steep cliffs of bare rock. These often rise above rock platforms that extend out to the sea beneath the waves, forming the inshore edge of the continental shelf.

▲ CAVES AND ARCHES
The higher a rock is above sea level, the less it is affected by waves, so if it is strong it may survive to form the roof of a cave or even a rock arch. Eventually, however, erosion cuts away the rock supporting it, and it comes crashing down into the sea.

▲ STACKS
The stumps of collapsed rock arches often form isolated stacks that are cut off from the land at high tide. Since they are usually made of particularly hard rock, they often survive for many years, while the rest of the coast is steadily cut back by erosion. They are frequently colonized by breeding seabirds because they are safe places to nest.

▲ WAVE ENERGY
Breaking waves drive water into cracks in the rock, forcing it apart. This loosens the rock and it falls away, often creating caves. The caves then collapse, leaving sheer cliffs that are attacked by more waves. This erosion process is most violent on shores that are exposed to strong winds and big waves. Soft rocks also erode faster, creating bays between headlands of harder rock.

◄ SHINGLE AND SAND
The rubble that falls in the sea is tossed around and smashed up to form boulders, shingle, and sand. Big, heavy boulders stay where they are, but lighter stones and sand are carried away from exposed shores by the currents. They are swept into bays and tossed up on shore by the waves, forming banks and beaches that help protect the coast from violent storms.

## BEACHES AND SPITS

CRESCENT BEACH
Waves breaking at an angle toss stones and sand grains sideways. This process, called longshore drift, gradually extends the beach down to the next headland. It often creates beautiful crescent beaches like the famous Copacabana Beach in Rio de Janeiro, Brazil.

LONG BEACH
If there is no headland farther down the shore, longshore drift keeps moving the beach material along the coast. This creates immensely long beaches, like this one on the south coast of England. The beach is often backed by lagoons cut off from the open sea.

SPITS
A long beach may extend into open water to form a spit. The spit keeps growing across the river mouth as more beach material is moved down the coast by longshore drift. Shown here is the Clatsop Spit in Oregon. It stretches 2 miles (4 km) across the river mouth.

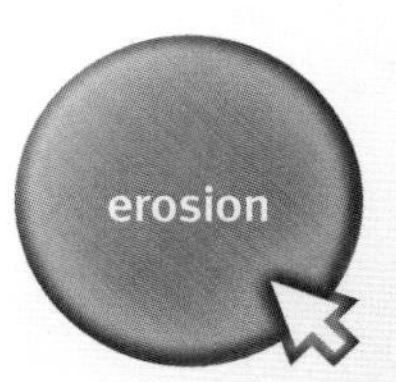


MUDFLATS ►
Mud particles carried off the land in rivers are dropped when the river current meets the sea, and they settle to form banks of fine, sticky, airless mud. These may extend to the sea to create a river delta, with several channels carrying sediments over its surface, as seen here in this satellite image of the Ganges Delta in Bangladesh.

# ABYSSAL PLAINS

The rocks of continents are constantly worn away by wind, frost, and rain, as well as by coastal erosion. Gravel, sand, and mud are carried off the land by rivers and swept into the sea. These sediments fan out from river mouths in the form of deep deposits on the seabed. Known as submarine fans, some cover huge areas and distort the Earth's crust with their weight. The sediments flow down canyons in the continental slope at the edge of the continental shelf, forming deep deposits at the foot of the slope. They spread out to form abyssal plains, which are vast flat areas of soft sediments on the ocean floors. These sediments also contain windblown dust particles, mud, and sand dropped by melting icebergs, and the skeletons of countless microscopic marine organisms that sink to the ocean floor to form thick layers of soft ooze. Over time the soft sediments harden into sedimentary rocks, and millions of years later major earth movements may raise these rocks to form new land.

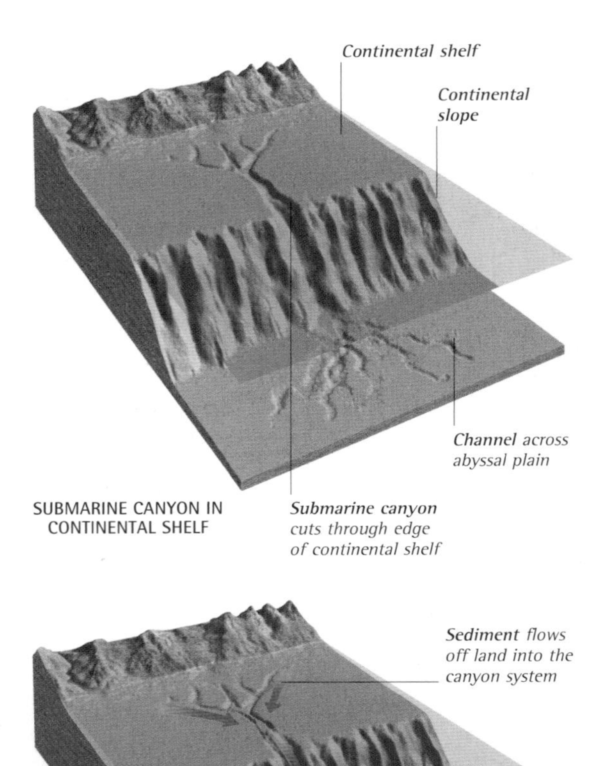


▲ MUDFLOWS AND CANYONS
Rock, sand, silt, and mud can cascade off the continental shelf in underwater avalanches called turbidity currents, especially during storms and earthquakes. These dense, heavy flows can scour deep canyons in the fringes of the continental shelf. Off the eastern coast of the US, for example, there are canyons 2,625 ft (800 m) deep. Submarine fans of debris spread out from the mouths of these canyons, forming the continental rise that links the base of the continental slope with the broad, flat abyssal plains of the deep ocean floor.

ICE RAFTS ►
In the polar regions, glaciers and huge continental ice sheets flow right down to the coast. They carry heavy loads of ground-up rock and shattered rock fragments that have been plucked from the underlying rock by the moving ice. The ice can be almost black with the minerals that it contains. When the glaciers reach the sea they break up into icebergs. These float away and gradually melt, dumping their rocky and muddy loads into the water, where it settles on the ocean floor. This process has helped to form the broad abyssal plains around Antarctica.

◄ AIRBORNE DUST
Huge quantities of airborne dust end up in the oceans and slowly settle through the water to add to the deep sediments forming the abyssal plains. A lot of dust is erupted from volcanoes, especially during catastrophic events like the 1991 eruption of Mount Pinatubo in the Philippines. The 1815 explosion of the Tambora volcano in Indonesia ejected so much dust that the sun was obscured for several months, causing the "year without a summer" in 1816. Much of this volcanic dust ended up in the oceans. Dust can also be blown off deserts, as shown in this satellite image of a storm carrying dust off the western Sahara and out over the Cape Verde Islands in the tropical Atlantic.

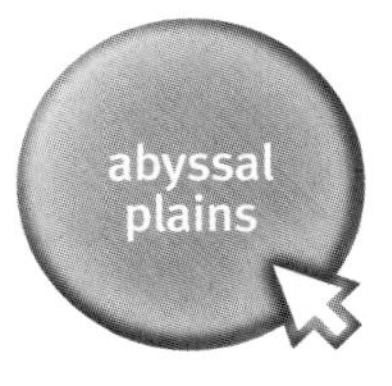


◄ BIOGENIC OOZE
Abyssal plains also consist of soft biogenic ooze, which is built up from the skeletal remains of microscopic marine organisms like these diatoms. But these dissolve in very deep water, so the main sediments on the deepest ocean floors are fine clays stained red by iron oxide.

SEDIMENTARY ROCKS

Over millions of years, ocean floor sediments are compressed into solid rock, which preserves in its characteristic layers a record of its formation. Many rocks have fossils of marine animals trapped in their layers, like these turret shells embedded in limestone. Each type of sediment turns into a different kind of rock: lime-rich oozes form limestone and chalk, sandy sediments form sandstone, and mud turns into shale. Dead organisms trapped within rock layers may not decompose properly, and through a long, complex process their carbon content can turn into the fossil fuels drilled from under the ocean floor by offshore oil and gas platforms.

# CHANGING SEA LEVELS

Sea levels are always rising or falling in relation to land. Ice ages affect sea levels by locking up water on continents as ice, and then releasing it into the oceans when the ice melts. The land rises when the heavy ice melts, and over longer periods it can be pushed upward by moving plates in the Earth's crust. As a result, sedimentary rocks formed on the sea floor are now found on land, and many coasts have features showing that the land has been submerged.

## CRETACEOUS OOZE

The pure white limestone known as chalk is made of the skeletons of millions of microscopic marine organisms. Known as coccoliths, they settled on the floors of tropical oceans during the Cretaceous Period, about 100 million years ago, forming layers of biogenic ooze. The soft ooze was compressed into chalk up to 1,300 ft (400 m) thick, then raised by ground movements to form the rolling hills and white cliffs of regions such as southern England, shown below.

MICROSCOPIC COCCOLITH

◄ RAISING THE ROCKS
Where sedimentary rocks have been uplifted, erosion often reveals the layers that were laid down on the ocean floor, along with the fossils preserved within them. Massive ground movements often buckle and fold these layers, as on this rocky coast.

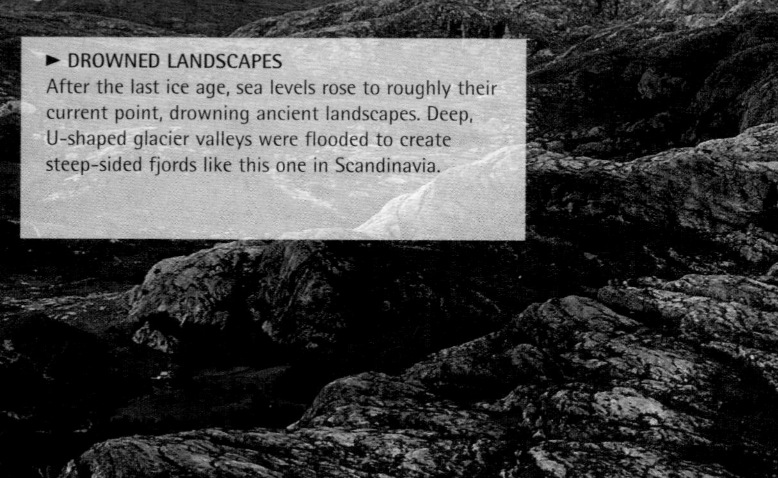

► DROWNED LANDSCAPES
After the last ice age, sea levels rose to roughly their current point, drowning ancient landscapes. Deep, U-shaped glacier valleys were flooded to create steep-sided fjords like this one in Scandinavia.

**RISING REEFS ►**
In many parts of the tropics, ancient coral reefs have risen above sea level as plateaus of coral limestone. One of the largest of these areas is northern Yucatan in Mexico. Here, there are no surface rivers, as the rainwater seeps down into a network of underground streams flowing through caves in the coral rock. At some places, the caves have collapsed to reveal beautiful pools called cenotes.

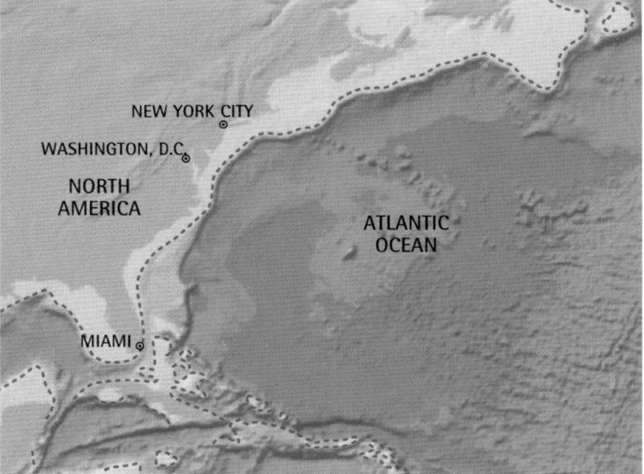


**◄ DRY SEAS**
During the last ice age, which ended some 10,000 years ago, world sea level fell by more than 400 ft (120 m), because so much water was frozen into huge ice sheets on land. This exposed the shallow continental shelves, and the continents became bigger. This map of North America shows the coastline as it was then, dotted red. Animals and people lived in areas that are now under water. Their remains are sometimes dredged up in fishing nets.

**▲ GLACIAL REBOUND**
World sea level rose after the ice age as meltwater flowed off the land. In places, however, the Earth's crust also started rising as it was relieved of the weight of the ice. This effect has raised ancient beaches well above the sea level, as in this bay in Wales.

# OCEAN WATER

Most of the water that fills the oceans originally came from inside the Earth. It was expelled from volcanoes as water vapor early in the history of the planet, and due to ideal conditions of temperature and gravity, this vapor eventually condensed into vast pools of liquid water that we call oceans. This ocean water is far from pure, since it contains many dissolved gases and minerals, including those that make it salty. It also contains the chemicals that form living molecules, making it likely that the oceans were the cradle of life on Earth.

*Water molecule*

*Hydrogen bond*

*Hydrogen atom*

*Oxygen atom*

▲ THE NATURE OF WATER
Water molecules are made of hydrogen and oxygen atoms. Weak electrostatic hydrogen bonds make the water molecules cling together as a liquid. At slightly higher temperatures, they drift apart to form a gas called water vapor. At lower temperatures, they lock into solid ice. Water is unique because these three states can occur in the same place, at the same time.

*Wind carries clouds inland*

*Water condenses into clouds as rising air cools*

*Plants lose water to the air*

*Water vapor rises from oceans*

*Water flows into ocean from rivers and streams*

*Water returns to ocean from ground*

◄ ICE
When the temperature of pure water falls below 32°F (0°C), strong hydrogen bonds lock their molecules together to form solid ice. Salty seawater freezes at a slightly lower temperature of 28.8°F (-1.8°C). Uniquely, the solid, icy form of water is slightly less dense than liquid water, which is why icebergs and ice cubes float.

◄ WATER
At temperatures above its freezing point, ice melts to form water. This is slightly denser and heavier, but the molecules are less tightly bound together. They can move around, and this is why water is a liquid. But the attractive forces between them are still strong, making water cling together in droplets.

◄ CLOUD
At 212°F (100°C), water boils and turns into water vapor, a gas. The water molecules break apart and float freely in the air. But this can also happen at lower temperatures, so water vapor is always rising off the oceans. It is invisible, but if it cools it condenses into droplets that form clouds.

▲ VOLCANIC ORIGINS
Nearly all the water on Earth was probably ejected from volcanoes when Earth's core was forming, more than 4.5 billion years ago. Volcanoes still produce vast amounts of water vapor and other gases, and this mixture would have formed an early atmosphere. The vapor condensed into rain that formed the first oceans. About 4 billion years ago, these may have covered the whole planet.

◄ WATER FROM SPACE
The comets that regularly enter the solar system are made of ice and dust. Hence, they are often described as "dirty snowballs." It is likely that many comets struck Earth during its early history, and the water from these comets melted and flowed into the oceans. Some scientists believe that this water from space may have contained complex molecules that formed the seeds of life on Earth.

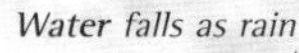



◄ THE WATER CYCLE
The sun-warmed surface water of the oceans is constantly evaporating, or turning into water vapor that rises into the air. Here, the vapor cools and condenses into clouds, which also contain other gases dissolved from the atmosphere. The clouds release rain that often falls on land. Water then flows off the land back to the sea, carrying dissolved minerals and sand, silt, and mud particles into the ocean.

▼ OCEAN CHEMISTRY
Water is very good at dissolving minerals and gases, which then form a part of its chemistry. These include carbon, oxygen, nitrogen, phosphorus, calcium, and iron—substances that are vital to animals, such as this crayfish, for tissue building and fueling body processes. Many of these substances remain on the ocean floor until the sediments are stirred up by strong currents.

▼ THE SALTY SEA
The water flowing off the land in rivers contains dissolved minerals called salts. The salt content in river water is so low that we think of it as fresh water, but in hot regions it often evaporates to leave thick salt deposits, like these at the edge of a salt lake. This occurs in the oceans all the time, and over billions of years, it has made ocean water salty. Most of the salt is sodium chloride, which is the same mineral as table salt.

# HEAT AND LIGHT

The oceans are warmed by the Sun, but tropical oceans are warmed far more than polar seas. Ocean currents redistribute this heat around the globe, which makes the polar regions warmer and the tropics cooler. Ocean water also warms up and cools down slowly, so it never gets as hot or cold as the land. Even sea ice is warmer than the ice formed on land. However, heat and light do not penetrate into the ocean depths, which are permanently cold and dark.

*Sun's rays dispersed and weakened near the poles*

*Sun's rays concentrated in the tropics*

**HEATING THE OCEANS ►**
The Sun shines down directly on the tropics, warming the surface water of tropical oceans to temperatures of 86°F (30°C) or more. Closer to the poles, sunlight is spread out over a broader area, weakening its power even in summer. The polar oceans get so little sunlight in winter that they freeze over, creating vast expanses of sea ice.

*Warm tropical water, with temperatures constantly above 77°F (25°C)*

*Temperate region of variable surface temperatures, ranging from 45–68°F (7–20°C)*

*Constantly cold polar water with surface temperatures of 32–37°F (0–3°C)*

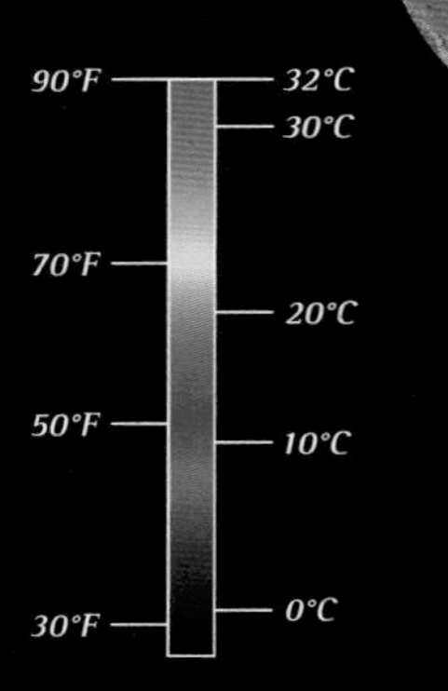


**◄ OCEAN TEMPERATURES**
The surface water of oceans is warmest in the tropics and coldest near the poles. But the water in the ocean depths is always just above freezing point, even near the equator. Despite this, the total range of ocean temperature is only about 104°F (40°C), compared to the temperature range of 295°F (146°C) on the continents.

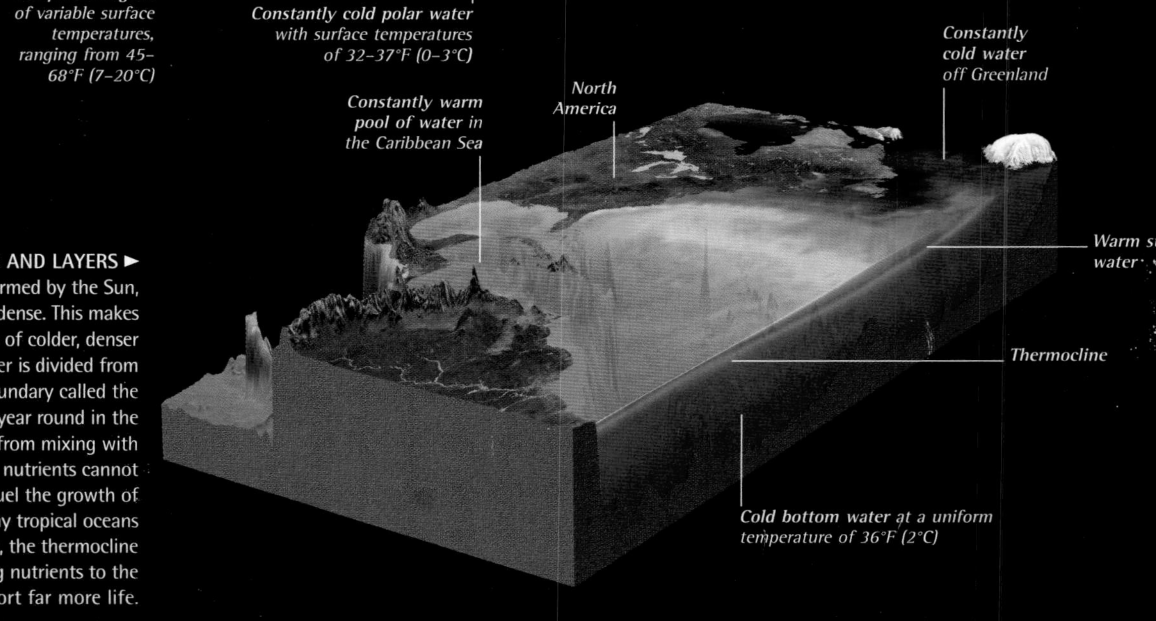


**TEMPERATURE AND LAYERS ►**
As ocean water is warmed by the Sun, it expands and becomes less dense. This makes it weigh less, so it floats on top of colder, denser water. The warm surface water is divided from deeper, cooler water by a boundary called the thermocline, which exists all year round in the tropics. It stops deep water from mixing with surface water. As a result, plant nutrients cannot reach the sunlit surface to fuel the growth of microscopic plankton. This is why tropical oceans are so clear. In colder oceans, the thermocline breaks down in the fall, allowing nutrients to the surface where they support far more life.

▲ LIGHT AND COLOR
Even in quite shallow water, everything appears very blue. This is because all the other colors that make up white sunlight are absorbed by the water. Red light is absorbed first, followed by yellow, then green and violet, until only blue light is left. At greater depths even this fades, leaving total darkness. This means that marine organisms that need light to make food, such as seaweeds and microscopic plankton, can only grow and multiply near the sunlit surface.

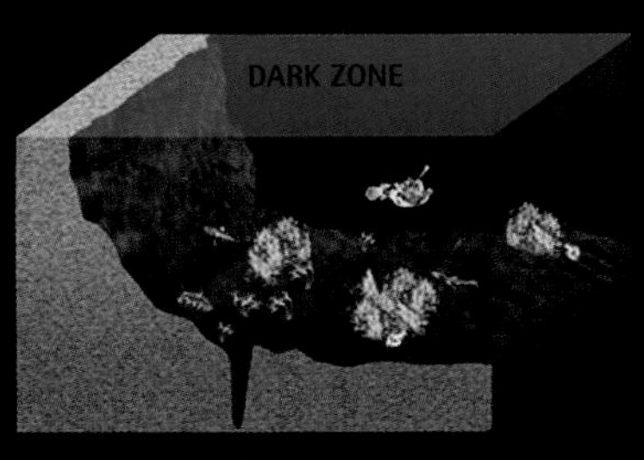


◄ LIGHT ZONES
The filtering of light by ocean water creates three main light zones. In the sunlit zone, there is enough light for seaweeds and plankton to flourish, and support other animals. Below 650 ft (200 m) is the twilight zone, where there is only dim blue light. Fewer animals live here, although many move down from the sunlit zone during the day. About 3,300 ft (1,000 m) below lies the dark zone, where there is no light at all except the strange luminous glow produced by many of the animals that live in the deep ocean.

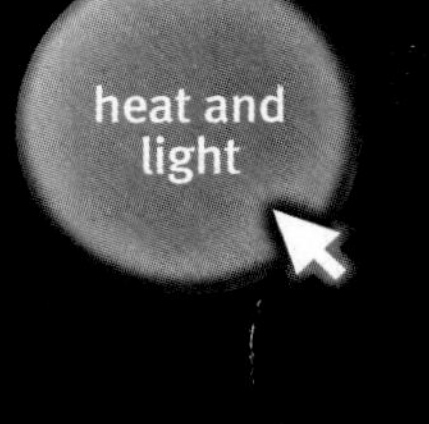


## PRESSURE

The enormous weight of ocean water exerts crushing pressure at depth. Humans are adapted to cope with atmospheric pressure, known as 1 bar. Just 33 ft (10 m) below the ocean surface, the pressure doubles to 2 bars, and at 65 ft (20 m) it increases to 3 bars. On the ocean floor, 10,000 ft (3,000 m) below the surface, it increases to some 400 times normal atmospheric pressure. This means that divers who work at depths below 165 ft (50 m) must wear special pressure-proof suits like this one. Manned submersibles designed to reach the dark zone have to be extremely strong, with the crew traveling inside a metal sphere that is designed to resist the colossal pressures that exist near the ocean floor.

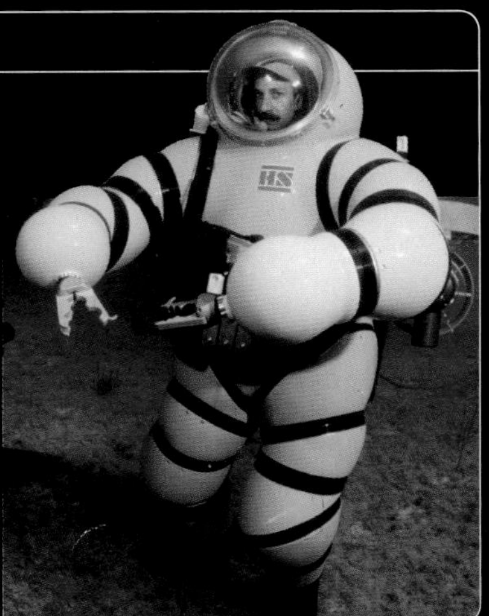

▲ SOUND
Sound travels through water five times faster than through air, and this enables whales, for example, to communicate over great distances. Sound transmission is most efficient at depths of around 3,300 ft (1,000 m) in a region called the SOFAR (Sound Fixing and Ranging) channel. Any sound generated within this zone cannot escape, but is reflected back into and along it. This focussing effect enables sounds to travel astonishing distances of up to 15,500 miles (25,000 km).

# ICY OCEANS

In the polar regions, the sea freezes where it is in contact with the extremely cold air. The ice floats at the surface instead of sinking to the ocean floor, because although it is colder than water, it is less dense. It can cover vast areas of ocean, creating the shifting, frozen world of pack ice. The ice cover expands in the dark, bitterly cold polar winter, and this affects the temperature, saltiness, and density of the ocean water below. But a lot of the ice melts away in summer when there is almost constant daylight, allowing light to flood the polar oceans and trigger an explosion of marine life.

▲ FLOATING ICE
As water cools it gets more dense and heavy, so it sinks. However, when it turns to ice, it grows less dense and floats, because its molecules spread to form a rigid hexagonal lattice, like honeycomb. In the process they expel salt, so the water in sea ice is almost fresh.

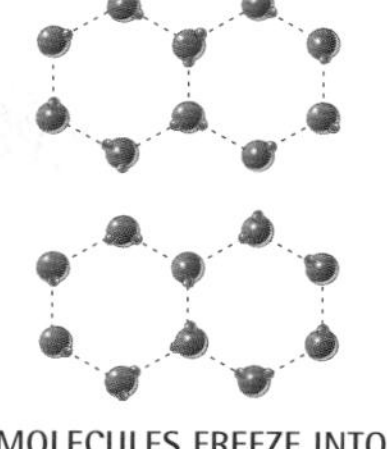

MOLECULES FREEZE INTO CRYSTAL LATTICE

## ICE FORMATION AT SEA

As the polar winter approaches, air temperatures fall and make water at the sea surface freeze into small crystals of frazil ice. If these are not dispersed by waves they gradually congeal into soupy grease ice.

As temperatures keep falling, the ice forms a thin layer at the surface. Water movement makes this break up into small rafts that rub together and develop the raised edges of pancake ice.

Eventually, the pancake ice freezes into a solid sheet, which gets steadily thicker all winter. During the following summer the sheet breaks up into large ice floes that drift with the winds and currents as pack ice. These floes often get pushed together to form a continuous, tumbled mass of floating ice.

GREASE ICE

PANCAKE ICE

PACK ICE

► ICEBREAKERS
In the Arctic Ocean, massive reinforced icebreakers plow through the sea ice to maintain corridors of open water for shipping. They ride up over the ice and smash it with their immense weight. They cannot deal with really dense pack ice, however, so they have to keep breaking the ice to stop it from growing too thick.

▲ DRIFTING FLOES
In some places like the central Arctic Ocean, pack ice form dense masses that are often piled into pressure ridges. Yet even these apparently solid sheets of ice keep moving. When Ernest Shackleton's (1874–1922) *Endurance* was trapped in the thick pack ice of the Antarctic Weddell Sea in 1915, the ship drifted 800 miles (1,300 km) with the ice before it was crushed and destroyed.

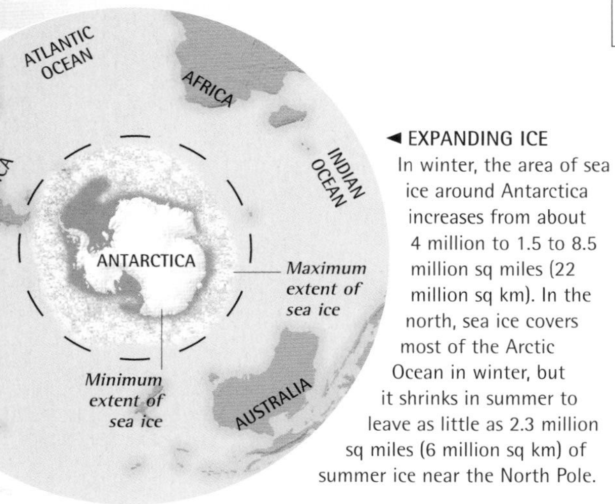


◄ **EXPANDING ICE**
In winter, the area of sea ice around Antarctica increases from about 4 million to 1.5 to 8.5 million sq miles (22 million sq km). In the north, sea ice covers most of the Arctic Ocean in winter, but it shrinks in summer to leave as little as 2.3 million sq miles (6 million sq km) of summer ice near the North Pole.

## THE WATER BELOW

Sea ice insulates the water below from extremely low winter air temperatures, but there is virtually no light because of the ice cover and the dark polar winter. Salt expelled by ice formation makes the water more dense, so it sinks. This forces deeper, nutrient-rich water to the surface, fueling the growth of marine life when the ice thaws. The sinking water also drives deep-water currents, and draws surface currents toward the polar regions.

▲ **ICEBERGS**
Where glaciers reach the sea, big slabs of ice break off and float away as icebergs. In 2000, an iceberg the size of the state of Connecticut broke away from the Ross Ice Shelf in Antarctica. Most icebergs are smaller, but since 90 percent of their bulk is underwater, they are all bigger than they look.

# OCEANS AND THE ATMOSPHERE

The heat of the Sun makes water evaporate from oceans and rise into the air as water vapor. The vapor then cools to form clouds and rain. This evaporation effect is most intense near the equator, where it creates a zone of huge storm clouds and heavy rain. The rising air is replaced by air drawn in from farther north and south, where cooler air is sinking. This airflow creates prevailing winds that blow across the tropical oceans. The Earth's rotation makes these tropical winds swerve toward the west. Meanwhile, air drawn toward the poles from the temperate regions sweeps eastward. These prevailing winds carry weather systems with them, and in many regions they have a big influence on climate.

▲ RISING VAPOR
About 100,000 cubic miles (425,000 cubic km) of water evaporates from the oceans each year. The water vapor mixes with warm air above the oceans, which tends to rise above colder, denser air. When the air rises it expands and cools down. This makes the vapor condense into tiny water droplets that form clouds and rain.

POLAR CELL

*Cold air sinks over the Arctic and flows south*

*Low-level air flows north in temperate zone*

FERREL CELL

*Air sinks over the subtropical desert zone*

*Dry desert air flows south*

HADLEY CELL

*High-level tropical air carries heat north*

HADLEY CELL

FERREL CELL

POLAR CELL

*Cool air sinks over Antarctica*

◄ CIRCULATING CELLS
When the warm air rising off tropical oceans reaches a height of about 10 miles (16 km), it meets the warmer air of the stratosphere, and stops rising. Pushed aside by more rising air, it flows north and south before cooling and sinking over the subtropics. Near the surface it is pushed aside by the sinking air. Some flows back toward the equator, replacing the air rising there to form a circulating Hadley cell. A similar circulation occurs in the polar regions, and these tropical and polar cells are linked by Ferrel cells flowing in the opposite direction.

THE SPINNING PLANET

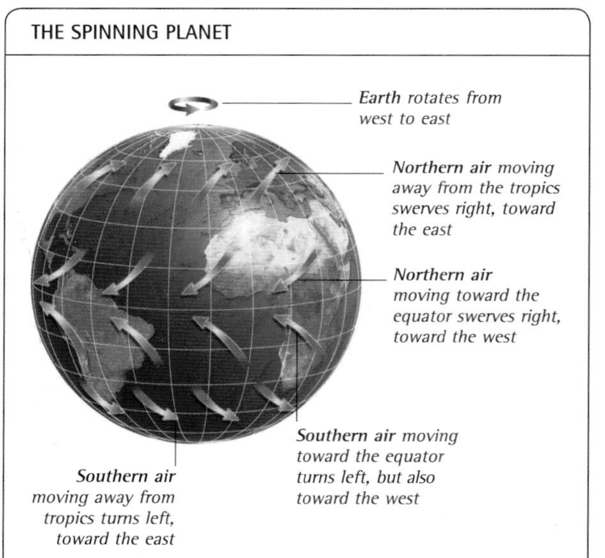


The airflow in the lower parts of the circulating cells causes the winds. If the planet was not spinning, winds would blow directly north or south, away from the zones of sinking air toward regions where warm air is rising. But the Earth's spin pushes the airflow off-course. Air moving toward the equator swerves west, while air moving toward the poles swerves east. This is called the Coriolis effect. It creates the global pattern of prevailing winds that blow over the oceans.

## PREVAILING WINDS

TRADE WINDS
The prevailing winds over the tropical oceans are gentle breezes that blow from the northeast or southeast. They are known as the trade winds, because in the days of sailing ships they were used by ocean traders sailing westward. To cross the Atlantic to America, for example, ships sailed south to the tropical islands off Africa, where they picked up the trade winds that took them toward the west.

WESTERLIES
Sailing ships returned east by heading away from the tropics to the temperate zones, to pick up southwesterly or northwesterly winds that would carry them back across the ocean. These westerlies are generally much stronger than the trade winds, especially in the far south where there are no continents to disrupt the airflow. Between 40°S and 50°S they are so strong that they are known as the Roaring Forties.

POLAR EASTERLIES
Near the poles, the prevailing winds blow south off the polar ice and swerve to the west. These polar easterlies drive floating pack ice westward around the Arctic Ocean, and westward around the coasts of Antarctica. In the Antarctic Weddell Sea, the westward flow swirls north along the shores of the Antarctic Peninsula, carrying the ice into the westerly wind zone where it is driven east again.

▲ CALM ZONES
Regions where the air is rising or sinking have very light winds, and often no wind at all. The zones of rising air near the equator are called the doldrums. These calm zones were once a problem for sailing ships, which could be stuck in them for weeks.

▼ MARITIME CLIMATES
Where prevailing winds blow off oceans onto the land, they carry moist air with them. In Ireland, for example, prevailing westerlies create damp, cool conditions that are ideal for lush grass growth.

# CYCLONES AND HURRICANES

Where a warm, moist air mass moving off an ocean meets a cold, dense air mass, the warm air rises above the cold air. This creates a swirling zone of rising air called a cyclone or depression. As the warm air rises it cools, so its moisture turns into clouds and rain. In temperate regions, prevailing winds carry these cyclones eastward, causing wet, windy weather. In the tropics, intense heat can generate the violent storms known as tropical cyclones, typhoons, or hurricanes.

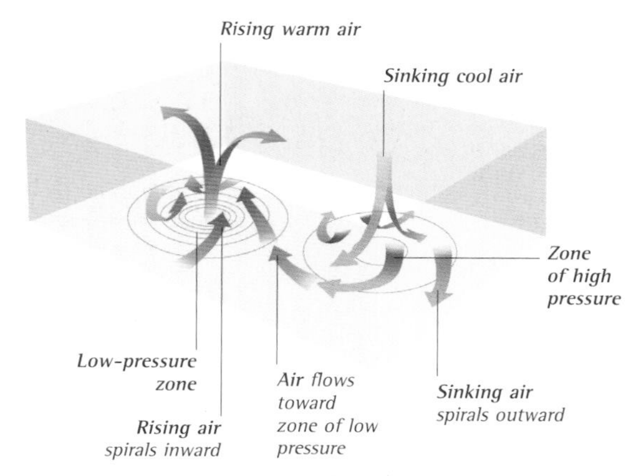


◄ HIGHS AND LOWS
Cool air is denser and heavier than warm air, so it tends to sink, pushing down to create a zone of high atmospheric pressure. It spirals outward as it sinks, swirling clockwise north of the equator, and counterclockwise in the south. It flows toward low-pressure zones, where warmer air is rising, and spirals inward in the opposite direction. As it rises, the water vapor in the air turns to clouds and rain.

▲ PRESSURE AND WIND
The greater the pressure difference between nearby zones of high and low atmospheric pressure, the faster the air flows from one to the other. This causes strong winds, especially around low-pressure zones. They blow around the cores of these cyclones, often against the prevailing wind, causing the storms that lash cool ocean regions like the North Atlantic.

▲ SPIRALING CYCLONES
The weather in cooler oceans is dominated by spiraling low-pressure systems, or cyclones. Many form along the polar front where warm, moist tropical air meets colder, drier air from the polar regions. They move steadily eastward, carrying wind and rain with them. Similar but more intense cyclones develop over warmer oceans, like the Caribbean storm seen in this satellite image.

▲ STORM CLOUDS
Clouds form as moist, warm air rises and cools, and the water vapor within condenses into water droplets. This releases heat, warming the air in the cloud and making it rise higher. More vapor condenses, releasing more heat, building huge storm clouds that can be more than 4 miles (6 km) high and cause torrential rain.

▲ WATERSPOUTS
Rising air within a storm cloud causes swirling currents that can turn into a tornado. When this happens over the sea the updraft can suck water up into the cloud, causing a waterspout. Although less violent than a tornado, it can capsize or wreck boats, especially when it collapses and drops its load of water.

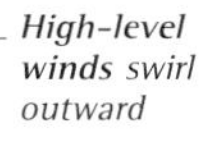

*High-level* ***winds*** *swirl outward*

*Low-level* ***winds*** *swirl inward*

***Strongest winds*** *spiral around the calm eye of the storm*

▲ HURRICANES
In tropical oceans where the surface temperature is higher than 81°F (27°C), vast amounts of water can evaporate from the ocean in fast-rising currents that create a zone of very low pressure. This makes the surrounding air swirl into the center of the system at high velocity, creating a revolving mass of huge storm clouds, torrential rain, and extreme winds—a hurricane.

STORM SURGE

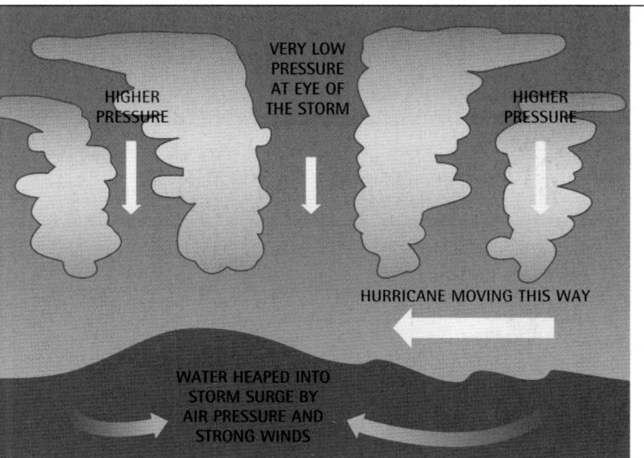


The atmospheric pressure at the eye of a hurricane is extremely low. This allows the surrounding higher air pressure and converging wind to push ocean water toward the core of the storm. It forms a mound of water called a storm surge, which is pushed ahead of the moving storm centre. If the hurricane approaches land, the storm surge heaps up in the shallow water like a tsunami, creating a wave that may be more than 33 ft (10 m) high. It was this effect that flooded the coastal city of New Orleans in 2005.

# WIND AND WAVES

Winds blowing over the sea whip the surface into waves. The stronger the wind, the bigger are the waves. Waves also grow as they travel, so the highest waves are those that have traveled great distances over broad oceans. They have great destructive power, especially on exposed coasts where breaking waves can splinter solid rock. Out at the sea, they cause less damage, although rare rogue waves may sink even big ships.

◄ WAVE ENERGY
Waves are caused by friction or drag as the wind sweeps over the ocean. The wind often blows the spray forward off the wave crests. However, the water within the wave does not move forward with it. Each water particle moves in a circle, rolling forward and then back as the wave passes. This action transfers the energy forward, which can become destructive when the wave finally breaks on the shore.

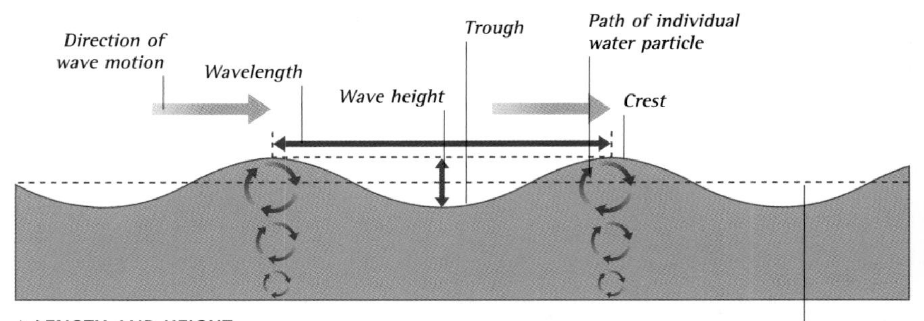


▲ LENGTH AND HEIGHT
Some waves are chaotic, especially if they are formed by strong winds or opposing currents. Most waves, however, develop into a regular succession of crests and troughs. The wave height is measured from trough to crest. The distance between each crest is called the wavelength, while the time delay between them is known as the period.

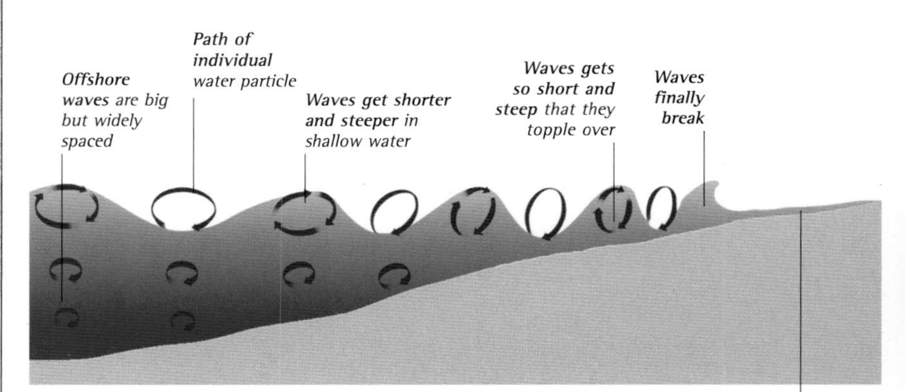


▲ BREAKING WAVES
As the waves approach the shore, the water becomes shallower. The waves become shorter and steeper as they are slowed down due to the interaction with the seabed. As each wave gets taller, it becomes less stable, and it finally topples forward to break on the shore. The steeper the shore, the more dramatically the waves break, releasing clouds of spray and driving a mass of water up the shore.

## WAVE DEVELOPMENT

RIPPLES
Ocean waves begin their lives as ripples on a flat sea, just like the ripples that are blown across a pond by the breeze. They are very small and close together, and from a distance they make the water surface shimmer without giving any impression of wave movement. If the wind keeps blowing, however, the ripples can grow into bigger waves.

CHOP
Ripples grow bigger and develop into a confused choppy sea, with waves up to 20 in (50 cm) high. The distance between the crests can vary from 10 ft (3 m) to 40 ft (12 m). They interact with each other to create a chaotic effect. These disordered waves are typical of areas where the waves are being whipped up by strong winds.

SWELL
The disordered chop of the sea becomes a regular series of waves called a swell. Though the distance between crests is much more predictable, the waves can grow higher if the wind is still blowing and the waves are able to travel over a big ocean. The swell seen here is breaking on the shore.

▲ PLUNGING BREAKERS
The farther a wave travels, the bigger it gets. The biggest waves occur in the Southern Ocean, where strong winds sweep them eastward around Antarctica. But some also head north into the Pacific. They may grow to be 60 ft (18 m) high by the time they reach the steep shores of Hawaii, which transform them into huge plunging breakers.

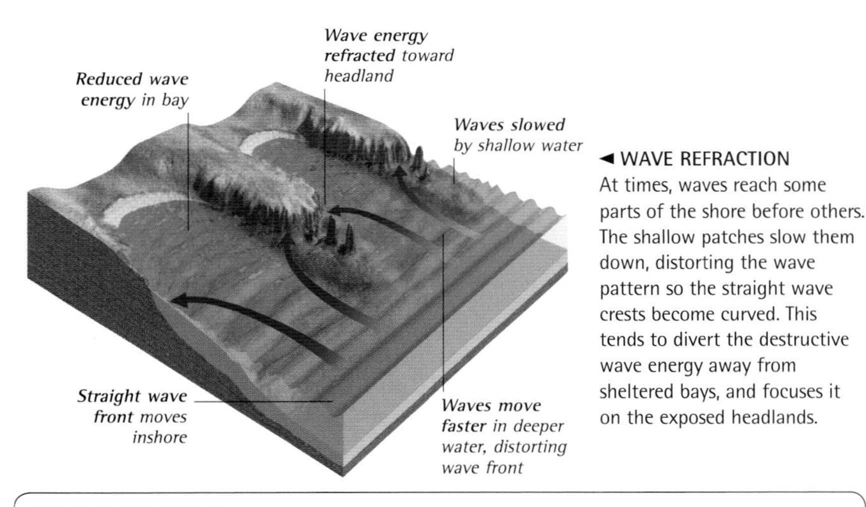


◄ WAVE REFRACTION
At times, waves reach some parts of the shore before others. The shallow patches slow them down, distorting the wave pattern so the straight wave crests become curved. This tends to divert the destructive wave energy away from sheltered bays, and focuses it on the exposed headlands.

## DESTRUCTIVE POWER

When a wave breaks, most of its mass topples forward with tremendous force. In a major storm, this force can reach up to 6,000 lb per sq ft (30,000 kg per sq m). On some shores much of this energy is absorbed by banks of shingle originally thrown up by the waves, so these act as natural breakwaters. On others, however, there may be nothing to stop the full force of the breaking waves slamming into coastal structures and cliffs. Over time, whole towns may disappear as the rock beneath them is swept away by the sea.

▲ ROGUE WAVES
Out at sea, regular swells can be quite high without being particularly dangerous. But if two swells with different wavelengths come together, they form a more complex wave pattern. This has flat spots where the wave troughs of one swell coincide with the crests of another, but has extra-large waves where two wave crests reinforce each other, as seen here. Occasionally, colossal waves form where opposing storm waves meet. These may be as high as 100 ft (30 m), and they often have breaking crests. Such rogue waves have been known to sweep right over huge ships, causing immense damage. They are probably responsible for many ships being lost without a trace.

# TIDES AND TIDAL STREAMS

Coasts and coastal waters in most parts of the world are strongly affected by the rhythm of the tides. These are caused by the gravity of the Moon constantly drawing ocean water toward it while the Earth spins. They are modified by other forces, including the gravity of the Sun. Tides are also influenced by the shape of the shoreline, which creates extreme tidal effects on some coasts, while others are almost tideless.

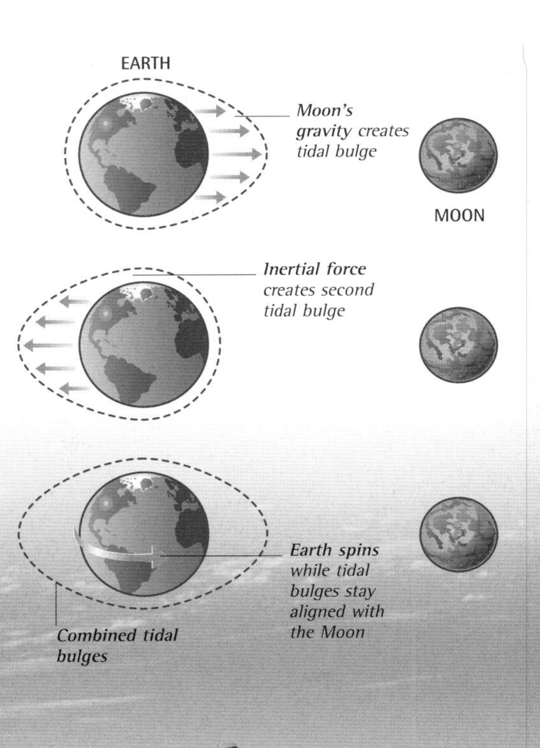


**LUNAR ATTRACTION ►**
As the Moon orbits the Earth, its gravity attracts ocean water to create a tidal "bulge." But the Moon's movement also makes the Earth move in space, slinging water away from the Moon to create another tidal bulge. As the Earth spins, its coasts move in and out of the tidal bulges, causing high and low tides.

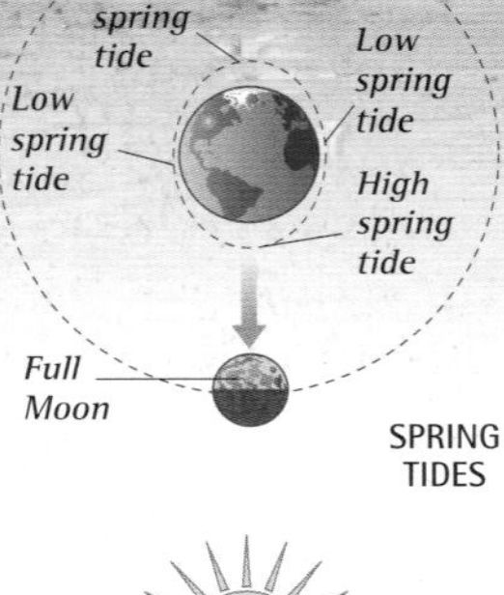


**▲ DAILY CYCLES**
If the entire planet were covered by oceans, the two tidal bulges would cause two equal high tides and low tides every day, with the time of high tide advancing by about 50 minutes every 24 hours as the position of the orbiting Moon changes. This is exactly what happens on many coasts. But the continents interfere with the smooth passage of the tidal bulges over the spinning Earth, giving some regions unequal tides. The shores of northern Vietnam, for example, experience just one tidal cycle a day.

**◄ MONTHLY CYCLES**
As the Moon orbits the Earth, it moves in line with the Sun twice a month at the times of full Moon and new Moon. When the Sun and Moon are aligned like this, their combined gravity causes extra-large spring tides every two weeks. In the weeks between a full and new Moon, the gravity of the Sun offsets that of the Moon, reducing the tidal bulge effect and causing less dramatic neap tides.

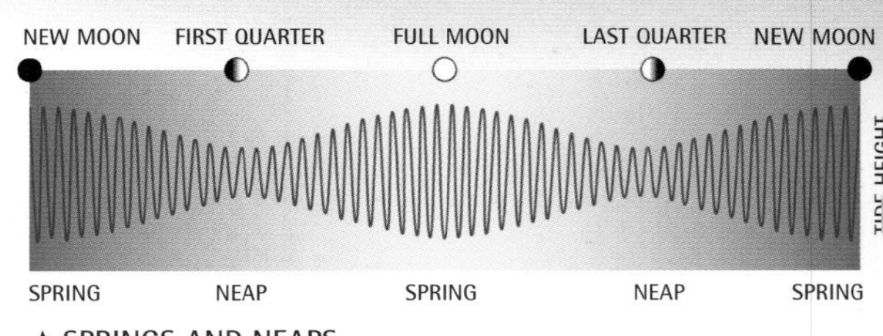


**▲ SPRINGS AND NEAPS**
The monthly cycle of spring tides and neap tides affects the total range of the tide, and not just its maximum height. A spring tide falls much lower than a neap tide, exposing more of the shore, as well as rising much higher a few hours later. The tidal range changes every day, increasing during the week before a full or new Moon, and decreasing as the phase of the Moon approaches its first or last quarter.

◄ LOCAL TIDES
Tidal range is influenced by local geography as well as by the alignment of the Sun and Moon. Some coasts have huge tidal ranges that are caused by tidal water being forced into funnel-shaped bays and estuaries, and then draining away again as the tide ebbs. The record is held by the Bay of Fundy in eastern Canada, seen here at low tide, which experiences a maximum tidal range of 50 ft (16 m).

▲ LOWS AND HIGHS
As the tide floods into the Bay of Fundy in eastern Canada—shown at low tide at the top of the page—it can rise at a rate of up to 13 ft (4 m) an hour until the tide peaks just six hours later, as seen here. By contrast, tide levels on many other coasts barely rise at all, and in parts of semi-enclosed seas such as the Mediterranean, the difference between low and high tide is barely perceptible.

tides

## TIDAL STREAMS

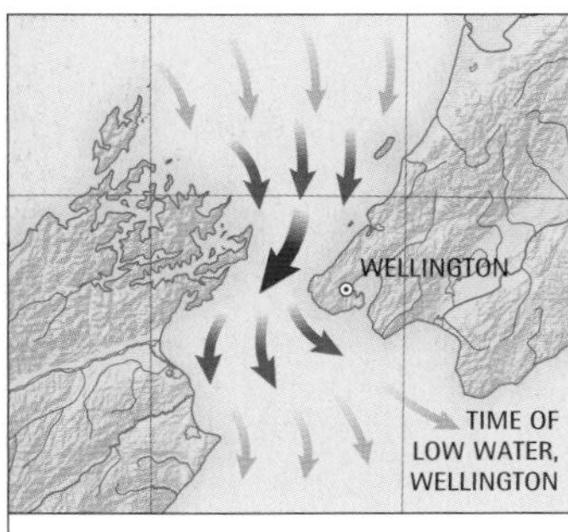


FLOOD TIDE
As the tide rises, water flows along coasts and floods into bays and river estuaries. These tidal streams can flow fast around headlands and through narrow straits, such as the Cook Strait between New Zealand's North and South Island. Such local tidal streams are often more powerful than ocean currents.

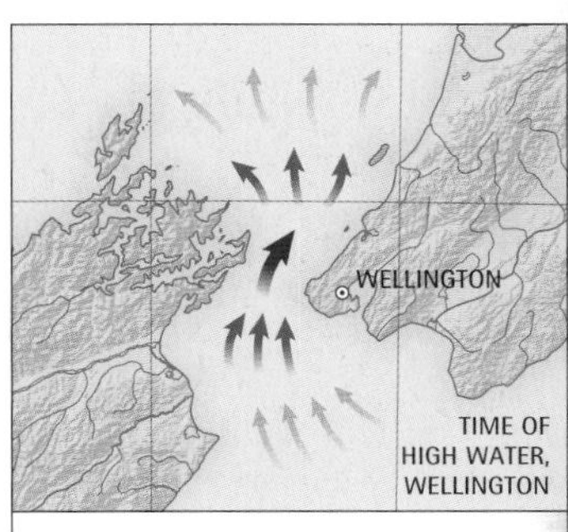


EBB TIDE
When the tide level starts to fall, water drains out of bays and estuaries in the ebb tide, and the direction of tidal streams along the coast reverses. In order to make their voyages possible, sailors have to know when these reversals occur each day, so they can take advantage of favorable tides.

RACES AND WHIRLPOOLS ►
Strong tidal streams pouring through narrow channels and around headlands can cause tidal races—fast, turbulent flows marked by whirlpools and steep, breaking stopper waves that stay in place as water flows through them. This whirlpool is a spin-off from the Saltstraumen tidal race on the northwestern coast of Norway, one of the most powerful tidal races in the world.

# SURFACE CURRENTS

The winds that sweep over the world's oceans drag the surface waters along with them, helping to drive the surface currents that flow around the oceans. The most influential of these winds are the prevailing winds generated by global air circulation. Deflected by the Earth's spin, they swerve toward the west in the tropics and toward the east in the temperate zones, driving the water in similar directions. The resulting surface currents form huge, swirling gyres that redistribute warm and cold water around the globe.

▲ **OCEAN RIVERS**
Surface currents flow like immense rivers through surrounding ocean waters. The Gulf Stream, for example, transports water northeast through the North Atlantic at some 1,766 million cubic feet (50 million cubic meters) a second—thousands of times the flow rate of the Amazon River in South America. This view from space shows the boundary between the fast-moving Gulf Stream at the bottom of the picture, and the coastal waters of North America at the top.

*Wind*

*Drag on ocean surface*

*Water moves in this direction*

*Drag from layer above*

*Direction of water movement in lower layer*

*Drag*

*Water movement in even lower layer*

▲ **THE EKMAN SPIRAL**
Winds blowing toward the east don't simply push water eastward. The spinning Earth effect that makes the wind swerve off-course also makes moving water veer right to the north of the equator, or left to the south. The moving water drags deeper water with it, and this also swerves right or left. The result is a current sheer that increases with depth, called the Ekman spiral after its discoverer, Vagn Walfrid Ekman (1874–1954). The total effect is that surface currents flow at about 45 degrees to the wind direction.

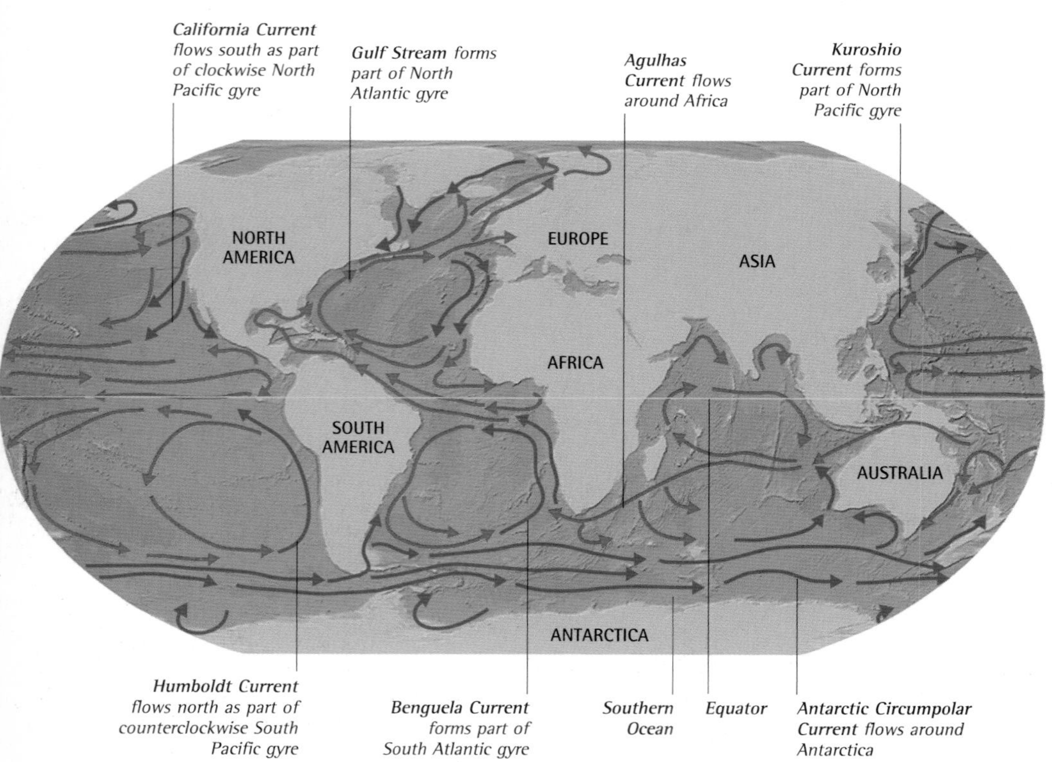


◄ **SWIRLING GYRES**
The combination of prevailing winds and the Ekman effect carries surface water westward near the equator, and toward the east in the temperate regions. In the Southern Ocean, the eastward flow continues around Antarctica, but elsewhere the continents force the currents to form ocean-scale circulations called gyres. These flow in opposite directions north and south of the equator, while offshoots of the main gyres flow into the Arctic Ocean and around southern Africa.

◄ BOUNDARY CURRENTS
Equatorial currents flow westward in the Atlantic and Pacific, so ocean water tends to pile up against the continents. This forces warm water north and south away from the tropics in powerful western boundary currents such as the Gulf Stream and the Kuroshio Current. These flow faster than the broader, less concentrated eastern boundary currents, such as the California Current and Benguela Current, which carry cold water toward the equator.

▲ WHERE CURRENTS MEET
Where warm and cold currents meet, the cold water tends to push beneath the warm water and stir up minerals from the ocean floor. These contain vital nutrients that fuel the growth of marine life such as plankton. Often the water in the two currents does not mix easily, as seen in this satellite view of the cold Falklands Current on the left, carrying green plankton, encountering the warm, southward-flowing Brazil Current carrying blue plankton.

## STILL CENTERS

The Ekman spiral pushes ocean water toward the still zone at the center of a current gyre, heaping it up in a broad, shallow mound. In the Sargasso Sea at the center of the North Atlantic gyre, the water level in the middle of the calm zone is about 3 ft (1 m) higher than the water level at the edge. The ocean surface is also covered with floating seaweed called sargassum weed, which has been concentrated in the Sargasso Sea by converging currents.

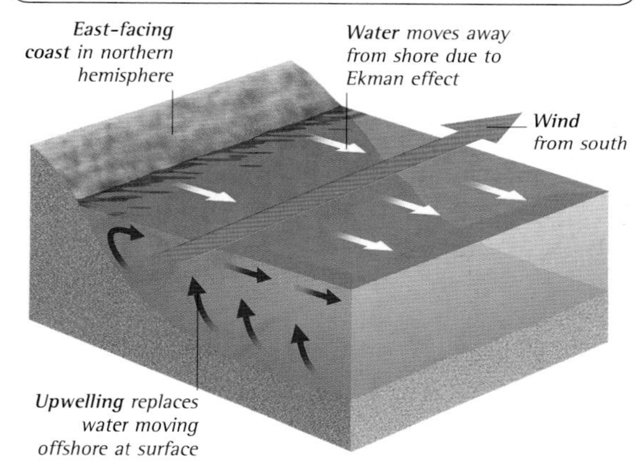


▲ UPWELLING ZONES
Where the wind and Ekman spiral drive surface water away from the shore, deeper water rises to take its place. This draws nutrients up from the ocean floor, causing blooms of plankton that feed marine life. These regions are called upwelling zones.

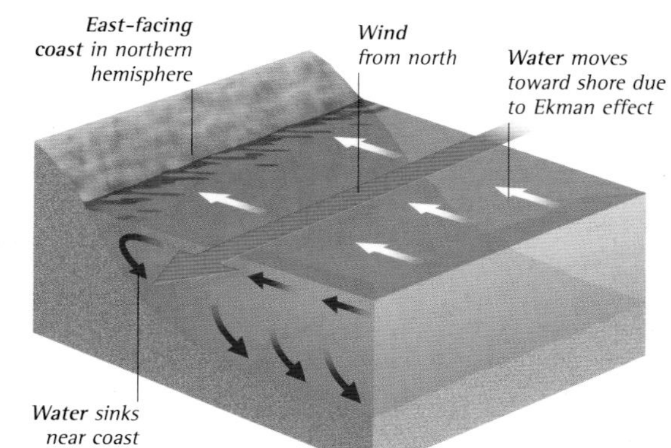


▲ COASTAL DOWNWELLING
The opposite of upwelling happens on coasts where the wind and Ekman spiral drive surface water toward the shore. This forces it to sink, suppressing the flow of nutrients toward the surface. As a result, there is little marine life in such downwelling zones.

# SEASONAL SHIFTS

Some oceans are affected by seasonal shifts in wind strength or direction, and these can weaken or even reverse their surface currents at certain times of the year. These changes are dramatic in the northern Indian Ocean, where the pattern of surface currents is changed by the regular wind reversal of the Asian monsoon. Another major switch occurs in the tropical Pacific, where weak prevailing winds may allow warm surface water in the western Pacific to flow east and suppress the normal current pattern, causing the climatic disturbance known as El Niño.

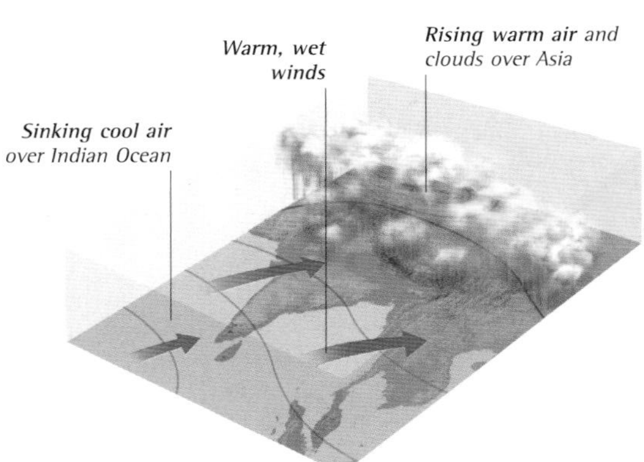


▲ SUMMER MONSOON
In summer, the huge landmass of Asia becomes much warmer than the Indian Ocean. Warm air above Tibet rises, drawing moist oceanic air from the southwest across India. Here, it rises and cools to form huge clouds over the subcontinent that cause the torrential rain and flooding of the summer monsoon.

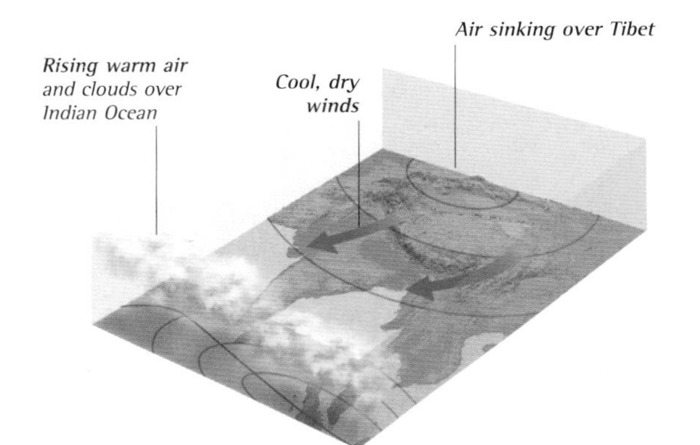


▲ WINTER MONSOON
In winter, Asia gets much colder than the Indian Ocean. This cools the air above Tibet, which sinks and flows southwest toward the warmer ocean where air is rising. It carries very dry air over India from the northeast, creating the dry conditions and cool winds of the winter monsoon.

MONSOON CURRENTS

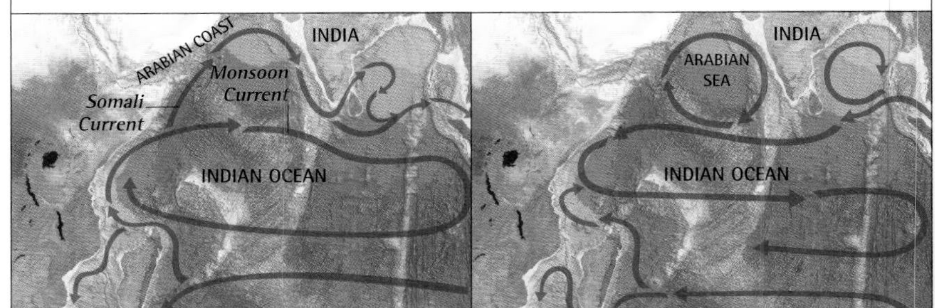


SUMMER MONSOON CURRENTS
Rising warm air over Asia in summer draws monsoon winds northeast over the ocean toward India. This drives the surface water of the northern Indian Ocean eastward in the Somali and Monsoon Currents. The strong winds also drag surface water away from the Arabian coast, making deeper, nutrient-rich water rise up to nourish the growth of abundant marine life.

WINTER MONSOON CURRENTS
When Asia becomes colder than the Indian Ocean the wind direction changes, so it blows toward the southwest. The switch reverses the current flow. The upwelling zone off the Arabian coast is suppressed as the wind blows surface water toward the shore, but the winds stir up the water of the central Arabian Sea to create another region of rich ocean life.

▼ RICH WATERS
Minerals stirred up by the monsoon currents supply nutrients to microscopic marine life, so it multiplies and provides rich food resources for fish and other animals. These support a local population of humpback whales that stay in the region throughout the year. The humpbacks seen here are feeding on fish by lunging up toward the surface with their huge mouths gaping open.

◄ EL NIÑO

The trade winds that blow over the tropical Pacific normally drive warm surface water toward the west. But every few years, this pattern is disrupted by a change in airflow that weakens the trade winds. This allows the warm water to flood back east toward South America, as shown in this satellite-generated image. The effects of this reversal are called El Niño, which means "The Child" in Spanish, because these events always occur around Christmas.

◄ NORMAL PATTERN

The pool of warm water that builds up around Indonesia and New Guinea warms the air above it so the air rises, carrying water vapor with it to generate huge storm clouds. The rising air flows east at high altitude, then cools and descends over South America, causing cloudless, dry conditions. Meanwhile, the westward drift of warm surface water draws cool, rich water up from near the seabed off Peru, creating an upwelling zone of abundant ocean life.

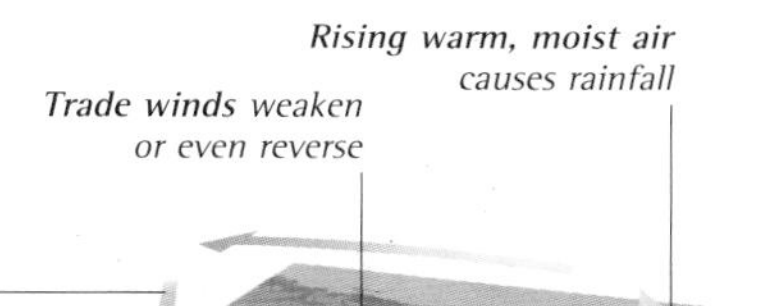


▲ EL NIÑO PATTERN

During an El Niño event, warm surface water flows back east. The warm flood blocks the upwelling of nutrient-rich water off Peru, so marine life either dies or moves away. It also brings stormy weather that causes torrential rains and floods in South America, while northern Australia and the islands of the western Pacific suffer from droughts and wildfires.

◄ DEVASTATED FISHERIES

The waters off Peru are among the richest fisheries in the world, with vast shoals of anchovies and other fish that feed on the marine life of the plankton. But the plankton swarms depend on cold, nutrient-rich water reaching the sunlit surface. When El Niño events prevent this, most tiny oceanic animals die. As a result, the fish that feed on them disappear, breeding colonies of fish-eating seabirds fail, and the fisheries that sustain local economies are devastated.

# DEEP-WATER CURRENTS

The surface currents that swirl around the oceans are linked to a network of slow-moving deep-water currents that carry ocean water all around the globe. Surface currents are driven by winds, but the forces that drive deep-water currents are more complex. The main mechanism is a change of density, caused by cooling and an increase in saltiness. This makes the water heavier, so it sinks toward the ocean floor. It then flows beneath warmer water, often very slowly, and gradually mixes with it until it returns to the surface. Eventually, this carries every gallon of ocean water around the globe, but the journey can take thousands of years.

*Salt expelled from ice is added to water*

***More surface water** flows in*

***Polar ice** cools the water below*

***Cold, salty water** sinks and flows away at depth*

▲ SINKING CURRENTS
Most of the sinking water that drives deep-water currents originates in the polar oceans, where floating ice and freezing at the surface make the ocean water colder, denser, and heavier. Salt expelled from ice also makes the water more salty, increasing its density. Due to the twin roles of temperature and saltiness, the mechanism is called the thermohaline circulation, after the Greek words for heat and salt.

***Open water** freezes in winter, cooling the water below*

***Pack ice** covers most of the Weddell Sea all year round*

◄ ANTARCTIC WATER
The coldest deep-ocean current flows from the Antarctic Weddell Sea, where the thermohaline process operates under the vast Ronne Ice Shelf as well as beneath the drifting pack ice. It creates a current called the Antarctic Bottom Water, which flows eastward across the floor of the Southern Ocean. It merges with a similar cold deep-water current, which is generated in the Ross Sea on the other side of Antarctica.

NORTH ATLANTIC DEEP WATER

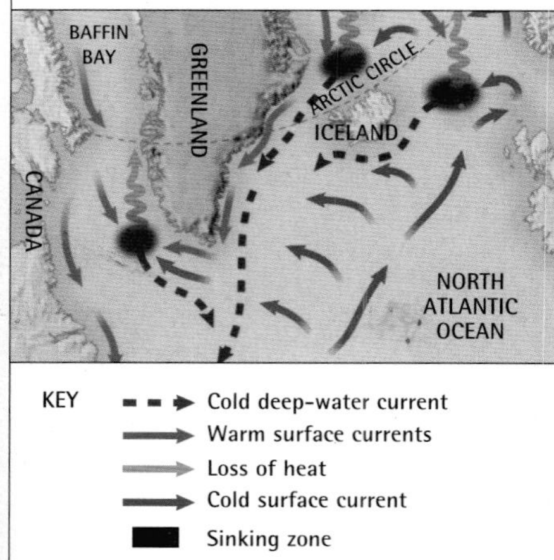


Most of the cold bottom water created by ice in the far north is retained by rocky barriers around the Arctic Ocean floor. But when warm, salty Atlantic water flowing north meets cold currents, it cools and sinks below the less salty Arctic water. The three main sinking zones drive a current called the North Atlantic Deep Water.

*Warm Gulf Stream flows north*

*Cold, salty water sinks in north Atlantic*

*Deep water rises up in north Pacific*

*Antarctic Bottom Water flows east*

*Cold, dense water flows north at depth into the Pacific*

**▲ THE GLOBAL CONVEYOR**
Cold bottom water flows through the Atlantic and Indian Oceans and into the Pacific. In the north Pacific and north Indian Oceans, some of it feeds into the surface current gyres. These link with surface currents in the Atlantic, where the Gulf Stream supplies the water that sinks in the far north to help drive the flow. This is often known as the global conveyor, because it conveys ocean water all around the globe.

**► SLOWING THE FLOW**
Global warming could weaken deep-water currents by reducing the amount of water sinking in cold oceans. This is partly because there is less ice forming on the ocean surface. But fresh water draining off the melting polar ice sheets into the sea also makes seawater less salty and dense, and less likely to sink. This is already reducing the flow of the North Atlantic Deep Water, which is the driving force behind the ocean conveyor.

**▲ VITAL SUPPLIES**
A vast amount of heat is moved around the world by the ocean conveyor. This helps prevent the cold polar regions from becoming even colder, and stops the tropics from becoming so hot that life there would be impossible. The deep-water circulation is also essential to marine life like these jellyfish, because it carries oxygen down to the ocean floors and draws vital nutrients up to the surface.

**▲ CLIMATE CHAOS**
If the global conveyor is weakened by climate change, it will affect the whole world, but the effect on northern Europe could be catastrophic. Sinking water near Iceland draws the warm Gulf Stream north, giving Europe its mild climate. If the Gulf Stream were to fail, European cities could suffer Arctic winters.

# NUTRIENTS AND LIFE

The ocean currents that move water around the planet also carry dissolved minerals that are essential nutrients for the simplest oceanic life forms—tiny plantlike organisms known as phytoplankton. Nearly all other marine life relies on these organisms for food, so in this way the nutrients support the entire oceanic ecosystem. Many of these nutrients are carried into the oceans by rivers. Some of the nutrients are soon taken up by marine life, but released again when the organisms die and their remains settle on the bottom. When ocean floor sediments are stirred up by currents and storms, nutrients are brought back to the surface. Here, the phytoplankton can turn them into food that supports the oceanic food chain.

◄ MAKING FOOD
Microscopic marine bacteria and phytoplankton contain a green substance called chlorophyll that absorbs the energy of sunlight. Using this energy, they combine carbon dioxide with water to make carbohydrates such as sugar and turn these into the tissues that animals use as food. Some deep-water bacteria make food in different ways, but for most oceanic life this process, known as photosynthesis, is the basis of life itself.

◄ VITAL NUTRIENTS
The tiny organisms that make carbohydrates by photosynthesis also need other nutrients. These include the nitrates and phosphates that are essential ingredients of proteins and the oxygen that turns sugar into energy. They need calcium and silica to build their shells and tiny, but essential, amounts of trace elements. Many of these nutrients occur in seawater, but they get incorporated into living things. When these die and their bodies decompose, like the remains of this turtle, the nutrients are released into the water—but many are stored in seafloor sediments until they are stirred up by ocean currents.

PLANKTON BLOOMS ►
Where vital nutrients are available, they nourish the growth of the microscopic plantlike organisms that form the phytoplankton. These tiny flecks of life drift in the sunlit surface waters of all oceans, but they are far more numerous where ocean currents bring abundant nutrients to the surface. In such places, the multiplying phytoplankton form dense plankton blooms that color the water and make it cloudy. They can cover vast areas like this swirling mass of plankton off northern Spain, which is at least 155 miles (250 km) across—and they are usually a sign of rich oceanic life.

## PHYTOPLANKTON

DIATOMS
In cool waters most of the phytoplankton consists of diatoms. These have shells of silica, which is basically glass. The shells fit together like microscopic boxes with lids, and they exist in a dazzling variety of forms. Most of the silicaceous ooze on the ocean floor consists of these silica shells.

COCCOLITHOPHORES
These tropical members of the phytoplankton have tough skeletons built up from tiny, ornamented disks of calcium carbonate or lime. When the organisms die and break up, the disks accumulate on the ocean floor as calcareous ooze. Over millions of years this may harden into limestone or chalk.

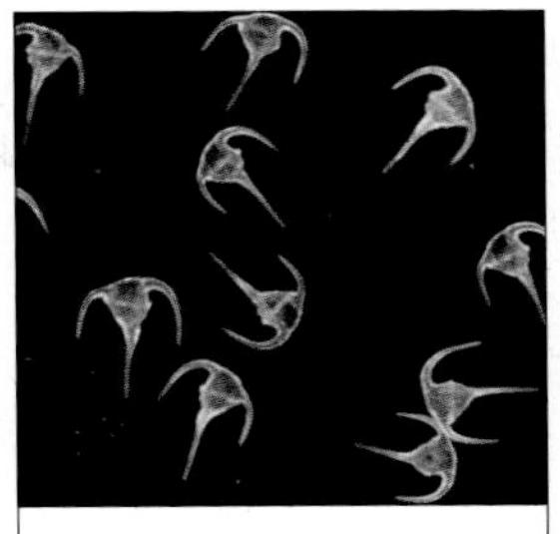

DINOFLAGELLATES
Like many microscopic organisms, dinoflagellates share features with both animals and plants. They are able to swim using tiny threadlike flagellae, but they make food by photosynthesis, like plants. Although they are a different shape, they have glassy silica skeletons, like diatoms.

### PHYTOPLANKTON DENSITY

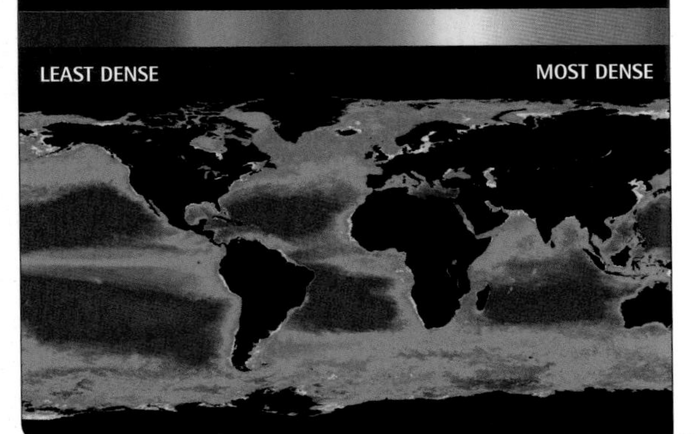


In tropical oceans, a layer of warm water stops nutrients reaching the sunlit surface zone, so phytoplankton cannot thrive. Upwelling currents overcome this near coasts, and in cooler oceans winter storms mix the water so phytoplankton can flourish. This satellite data shows that these waters are much richer than those of warm tropical oceans.

▲ SEAWEEDS AND SEAGRASSES
In shallow water, seaweeds do the same job as phytoplankton, using solar energy to make food from carbon dioxide and water. Some seaweeds do this so efficiently that they can grow at rates of 2 ft (60 cm) a day, and their fronds reach lengths of 165 ft (50 m) or more. They form the submarine forests of giant kelp that grow in the coastal waters of the east Pacific. Marine plants called seagrasses also grow in sheltered waters. They provide food for small animals that are eaten by fish, and they are also grazed upon by sea turtles.

TROPICAL CORAL REEFS ◄
Clear tropical oceans contain very little phytoplankton, but the corals that build tropical coral reefs have similar organisms living in their tissues. These make food in the same way as phytoplankton, and supply some of it to the corals. In return, the corals provide them with nutrients obtained by trapping small animals. The arrangement relies on plenty of light, so tropical coral reefs always grow in clear, shallow water.

# THE MARINE FOOD WEB

Nearly all life in the ocean depends on phytoplankton, which turn simple chemicals into complex substances that animals can use as food. The phytoplankton are eaten by microscopic animals, which are in turn eaten by slightly larger animals. They all drift and swim in the oceans as zooplankton. These plankton swarms are harvested by larger creatures like fish, which fall prey to hunters such as sharks.

## ZOOPLANKTON

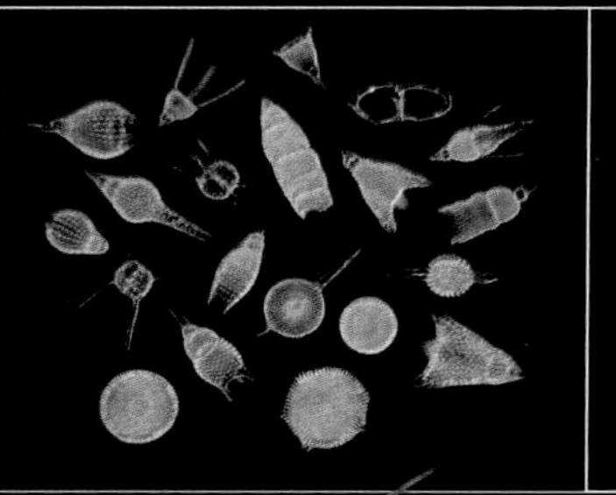

RADIOLARIANS AND FORAMS
These microscopic protozoans multiply fast among blooms of phytoplankton such as diatoms and dinoflagellates, which they catch by seizing them with threads of body tissue that they extend through holes in their shells. Radiolarians like these have shells of glassy silica. By contrast, forams have lime-rich shells that resemble tiny snails.

COPEPODS
Copepods are miniature crustaceans (shrimplike animals) that trap phytoplankton by straining water through their feathery legs. They form dense swarms in food-rich waters, providing prey for shoaling fish. At night they swim up toward the surface, where phytoplankton are most abundant, but they retreat to the darker, safer twilight zone at dawn.

KRILL
In the cold Southern Ocean around Antarctica, copepods are replaced by krill. These much bigger crustaceans feed in the same way as copepods, but they form larger swarms that can turn the ocean water red. They are the main food of most Antarctic fish, seabirds, penguins, crabeater seals, and whales, and without them the Antarctic ecosystem would collapse.

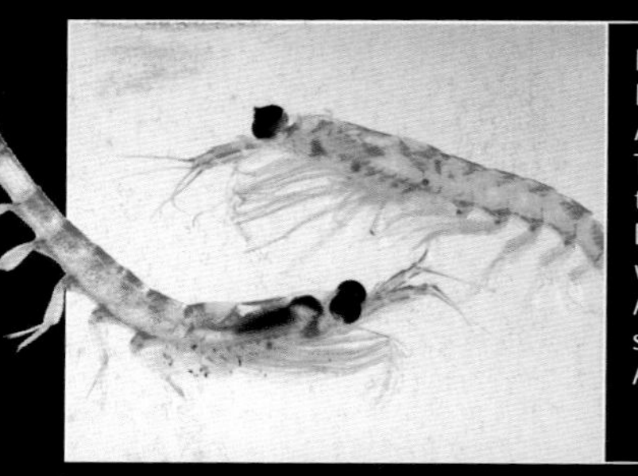

EGGS AND LARVAE
The drifting community of plankton forms a nursery for the eggs and larvae of many marine animals, including fish, mollusks, and crustaceans. When the eggs hatch, the larvae feed on plankton until they turn into small adults. Many, like these crab larvae, will then begin a completely different way of life, feeding on the seabed or even clamped onto rocks.

▲ DRIFTING JELLIES
All kinds of strange jellylike animals hunt among the plankton. Although many can swim, they mainly drift in the currents with their prey. They include jellyfish like this one, which is using its poisonous tentacles to trap copepods, as well as iridescent comb jellies and organisms called salps that look like long chains of plastic bags.

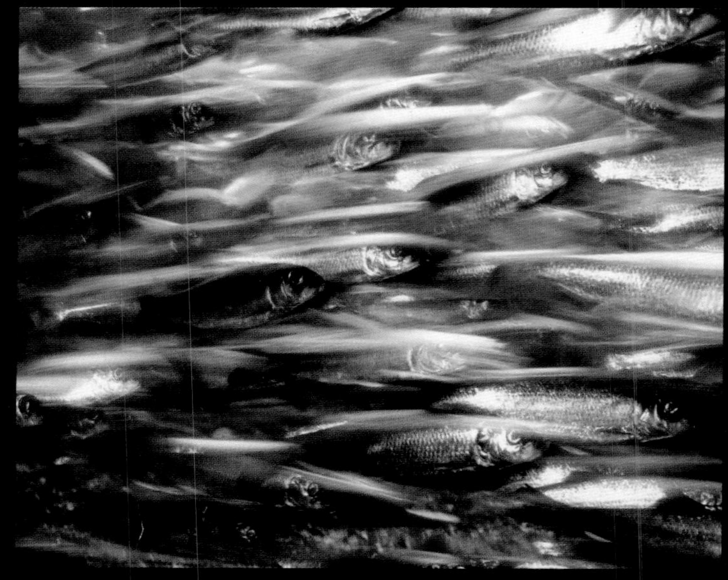

▲ HUNGRY SHOALS
Many small fish such as anchovies and herring feed by swimming through plankton swarms with their mouths open, so that the water flows through their gills. The gridlike gill rakers protecting their gills act as sieves, trapping plankton. These fish swim in dense shoals of thousands or millions, each shoal forming a superorganism that behaves like one huge animal.

**OCEAN HUNTERS ►**
Shoaling fish are hunted by a variety of predatory fish such as these tuna, as well as other hunters such as dolphins. These are fast-moving animals that patrol large areas of ocean in search of prey. Tuna and dolphins hunt in packs, but others such as marlins and swordfish are solitary ocean nomads that stay on the move throughout their lives, searching for prey.

**TOP PREDATORS ►**
The hunters are hunted themselves by formidable predators like the great white shark. Such predators are relatively scarce, because it takes many tuna to feed one shark, and huge numbers of small fish to feed all the tuna. The tuna also use up a lot of energy as they swim, rather than turning it into flesh that the shark can eat. This means that each shark must be supported by many times its own weight in small fish.

food web

**GIANT FILTER-FEEDERS ▲**
Some big fish eat very small animals, filter-feeding in the same way as shoaling fish. This is very efficient, because no energy is used up by intermediate feeders like tuna. It enables these animals to grow to immense sizes, and the filter-feeding whale shark seen above is the largest of all fish. Many whales feed in a similar way, and grow to a colossal size. The krill-eating blue whale, for example, is the biggest animal that has ever lived.

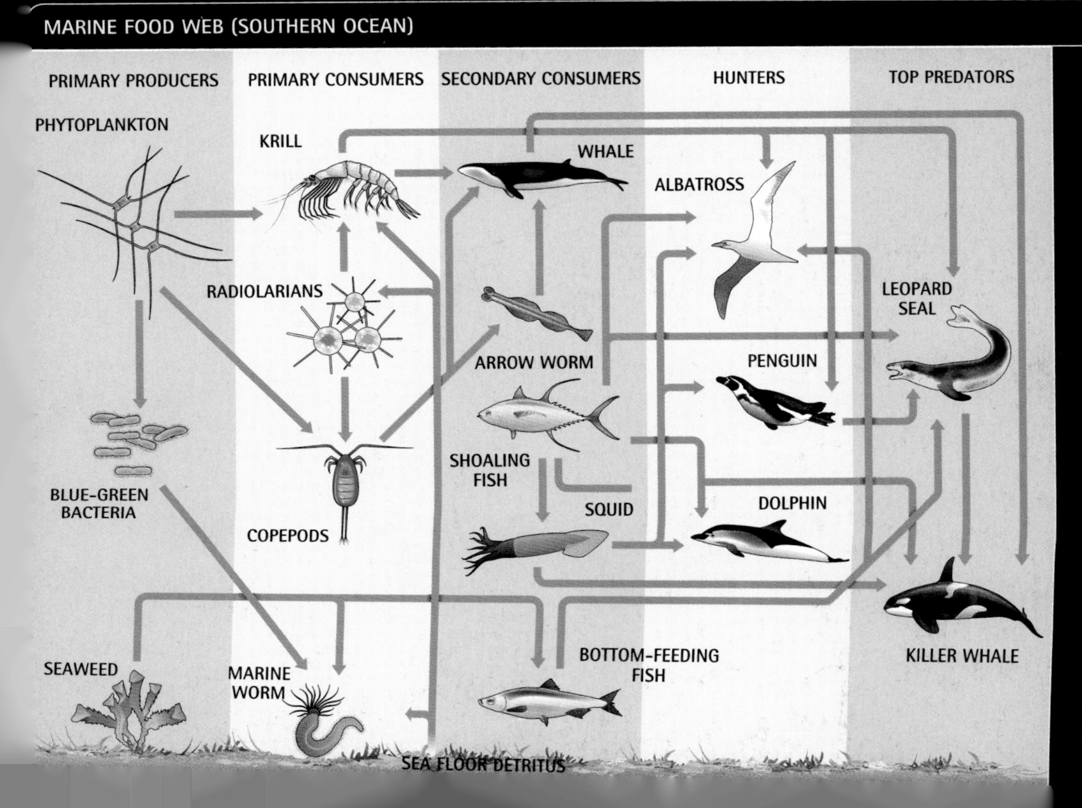


Every oceanic habitat has its own food web, which connects the primary food producers with the top predators. Basically, each animal occupies a different level in the ecosystem. Primary producers like phytoplankton are eaten by primary consumers such as copepods and krill. These are eaten by secondary consumers like squid and fish, which are hunted by animals such as penguins and dolphins. These may then fall prey to top predators like killer whales. Meanwhile, the remains of dead animals and plankton sink to the ocean floor, where detritus is recycled into essential nutrients by decomposers such as marine worms.

However, this oceanic food web for the Southern Ocean shows that the connections are more complicated. This is partly because most animals eat various kinds of foods. A killer whale, for example, will eat penguins when it gets the chance, but it also feeds on the squid and fish that penguins eat. It might also eat a leopard seal, which is another top predator that preys mainly on penguins. Giant filter-feeders like whales feed at the same level as tiny arrow worms, but they eat the arrow worms, too. Whales also have nothing to fear from hunters such as seabirds and penguins that occupy the next level.

Despite the complications, one thing is clear about all oceanic food webs. Every animal, big or small, depends on the food created by primary producers such as phytoplankton. If there are no primary producers there is no food, and no food web.

▲ SITTING TIGHT
Where food is plentiful because the water is rich in nutrients, marine creatures can make a good living by staying in one place and collecting any food that comes their way. Many animals, like these mussels, attach themselves to rocks and other solid objects, while others burrow into soft sand or mud, and extend feeding tubes or long tentacles to gather food.

# LIVING UNDERWATER

Living underwater is unlike living on land, because the moving water is full of drifting food. A huge variety of animals such as sea anemones, barnacles, and clams make the most of this by anchoring themselves in one place and waiting for the currents to bring food to them. More mobile animals actively search for food, but even these benefit from the way the water supports their bodies. Many are superbly streamlined, enabling them to swim efficiently, and some of their highly tuned senses work in ways that we find hard to imagine.

## GATHERING FOOD

FILTERING
A mussel draws water into its body through a siphon tube, filters it for edible particles, then expels it through a second siphon. Clams that burrow in soft sand feed in the same way.

STRAINING
Some marine worms spread fans of tentacles in the water to snare any edible items. Barnacles use a similar technique, extending feathery legs from "trapdoors" in the tops of their shells.

TRAPPING
The tentacles of some animals like this anemone are armed with tiny stings, which they use to immobilize and trap small animals. Venomous jellyfish use the same adaptation in open water.

SEIZING
Tropical garden eels sit with their tails in the sand and their mouths facing the current, ready to seize any food items that drift by. They live only in places where the current is quite strong.

◄ GLIDING AND CRAWLING
Many of the animals that attach themselves to the seafloor are eaten by other creatures that move over the bottom. Some, like these sea slugs with their violet-tipped tentacles, glide over the rocks to prey on attached animals. Sea snails, starfish, and sea urchins move in a similar way. Mobile crustaceans such as crabs and lobsters crawl about on well-developed legs, in search of prey and edible scraps. Most are weighed down by their heavy shells, but smaller shrimps and prawns can swim.

## UNDERWATER SENSES

VISION
Light does not penetrate far under water, especially if the water is cloudy, but many animals have good vision for both hunting and defense. An octopus has eyes like ours, and the scallops that it eats have simple eyes dotted around their shell rims to detect danger.

SMELL
Scent and taste are vital clues to the presence of food. Sharks are famous for the way they detect tiny amounts of blood in the water, and many carnivorous sea snails, like this one, locate their victims by sniffing them out with their long, sensitive snouts.

HEARING
Sound travels fast under water, and for very long distances. Many animals such as fish can detect such sounds even though they do not have ears. Dolphins exploit this by using bursts of sound to scare fish into dense groups, making them easier to catch.

PRESSURE SENSE
Many oceanic animals are able to detect pressure changes in the water. Fish pick them up through a line of sensors along each flank, called the lateral line. Pressure changes make them aware of movements nearby, and enable shoals to swim in perfect unison.

ELECTRO-SENSITIVITY
Some marine creatures such as sharks and rays are able to detect the faint electrical nerve signals of other animals. The electro-sensors that pit the snout of this shark enable it to locate even invisible, scentless prey with deadly accuracy.

▲ SWIMMING
The bodies of many marine animals have almost the same density as water. This gives them neutral buoyancy, so they can hang in the water above the seafloor. Most fish have inflatable floats that they use to adjust their buoyancy. Others, such as sharks, sink slowly unless they keep swimming. Open-water fish like these mackerel are highly streamlined, so they can move fast without wasting energy.

◄ DEEP DIVING
Some air-breathing sea animals are specially equipped for diving. They include mammals, like this sperm whale, that dive to extreme depths to seize fish and squid. The main problem for these marine mammals is surviving the intense pressure at great depth. This makes their lungs useless, so they have to store vital oxygen in their blood and muscles.

# LIFE IN SHALLOW SEAS

▲ SHALLOW FRINGES
The fringes of the continents are covered by sunlit seas that are generally less than 650 ft (200 m) deep. The shallow seafloors are covered with sand, mud, and other sediments that have been swept off the land by rivers and coastal erosion. These sediments are enriched with the remains of land plants and animals, as well as those of dead sea creatures, so they are full of the nutrients needed by marine life.

Most marine life lives in shallow seas, on the continental shelves that fringe the deep oceans. The shallow water makes it easy for essential nutrients from the seabed to reach the sunlit surface zone, where phytoplankton can use them to make food. The seabed itself may also lie within the sunlit zone, giving a wide variety of bottom-dwelling animals direct access to rich supplies of living food.

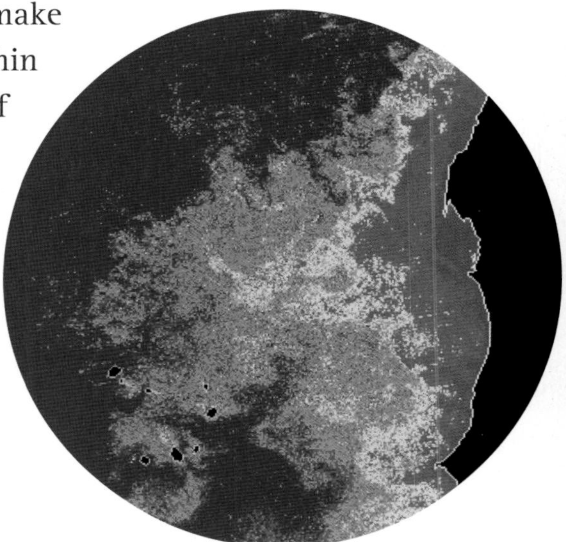

► SCOURING CURRENTS
Most nutrients that support the flourishing marine life of coastal seas are scoured up from the shallow seabed by storms and currents. This effect is most intense where surface currents moving away from the coast draw deep water up to the surface. This satellite image of the west African coast shows one of these upwelling zones, with red and yellow indicating dense clouds of multiplying phytoplankton.

## SHELF LIFE

ON THE BOTTOM
A lot of animals live on the seabed, either buried in the mud and sand or hidden among rocks and wrecks. They include burrowing clams and worms, attached animals such as mussels and sea anemones, and mobile starfish, sea urchins, crabs, crayfish, and lobsters.

NEAR THE SEABED
Many fish such as rays, flatfish, and this Atlantic cod feed on or near the seabed in shallow seas. There is plenty to eat, and prey animals such as crabs and burrowing clams are easy to catch compared with the fast-moving fish that live in the waters above.

OPEN WATER
The zooplankton that swarm in shallow, sunlit, nutrient-rich seas are preyed upon by large shoals of fish that swim in the open water well above the seabed. The fish and their prey move toward the surface at night, and back down into deeper water by day.

SURFACE DIVERS
Many animals that breathe air at the surface are able to reach the shallow seafloor very easily, and feed on the rich variety of prey that lives there. They include a variety of diving seabirds such as auks and cormorants, and mammals such as sea otters and seals.

◄ COASTAL WATERS
The shallow coastal waters of many cool oceans support lush beds of seaweed that are very efficient producers of food. Some of the most spectacular of these are the kelp forests that grow near the Pacific shores of North America. Here, giant kelp grows in water up to 165 ft (50 m) deep, yet extends its long fronds right up to the surface. The kelp fronds are grazed upon by armies of sea urchins, and these are eaten by sea otters that use stones to smash open the urchins' spiny shells.

► SEABIRD COLONIES
Vast coastal breeding colonies of seabirds rely on the rich waters of continental shelf seas to supply them with food to feed their young. These breeding colonies are particularly numerous near upwelling zones, such as near the coasts of Peru and Chile, and on the fringes of polar oceans where the spring thaw creates a sudden explosion of life in the cold green waters.

▲ RICH FISHERIES
For centuries the richest fisheries were found in the shallow continental shelf seas, which were also conveniently close to land. Intense fishing over the past century has virtually destroyed many populations of the most popular food fish, such as cod and herring. But these fertile waters are still capable of supporting huge fish shoals, and conservation and fishing restrictions may allow the fish stocks to recover.

# LIFE ON TIDAL SHORES

Water near the shore contains a lot of nutrients and drifting food, making the shoreline a rich habitat for marine animals. But it is also a very dangerous place. The breaking waves can crush any animal that is not concealed in crevices or burrows, and on tidal shores the falling tide exposes a region where attached animals such as mussels and barnacles risk drying up under the sun. The depth of this intertidal region changes every day, affecting what can live there, and this creates distinct shore zones inhabited by different types of marine life.

*Limpets clamp themselves to rocks, protected by their thick conical shells*

▲ DANGER AREA
As the waves crash on the shore, they pick up rocks and stones and toss them around. On rocky shores, animals can avoid the worst by creeping into crevices, which also prevents them from drying out as the tide falls. But most shore animals are very resilient, with extremely strong shells or tough rubbery skins.

SHORE ZONES ►
Different animals and seaweeds can survive different periods of exposure by the falling tide. The lowest parts of the shore are underwater nearly all the time, and are exposed only during low spring tides. The middle shore is covered and exposed every day, but the upper shore may be flooded for only a few hours twice a month, during high spring tides.

shoreline life

▲ LIVING WITH THE TIDES
Most tidal shore animals, such as these sea anemones, feed only when submerged. They survive low tide by closing up to retain water. Some do this more efficiently than others, so they can survive for longer and colonize higher zones of the shore.

◄ LIFE ZONES
Only a few types of animals can live above the lower shore, within tight limits imposed by the tide. But they multiply into dense colonies that form visible bands on rocky shores. On the far shore of this bay, massed mussels form a black band below zones of pale brown barnacles and yellow lichen.

▲ TIDE POOLS
On rocky shores, the receding tide often leaves pools of water among the rocks. When this happens high on the shore, the pools heat up and may dry out, but pools that form below midtide level are not exposed to the Sun for so long, so they stay cool. They make ideal refuges for marine life that cannot survive being left high and dry for several hours, and the biggest tide pools may even contain large fish.

▲ BEACH LIFE
Most of the animals that live on sandy beaches and tidal mudflats are burrowing clams and worms, which use tubes and tentacles to gather food from the water at high tide. There may be millions of them, but when the tide goes out they retreat into their burrows and are hidden from view. The shorebirds that feed at low tide know their hiding places, however, and are experts at digging them out.

## COASTAL PLANTS

ROCKY CLIFFS
In the splash zone above the level of high spring tides, the shore is colonized by flowering plants such as thrift. These maritime plants can tolerate being drenched in salt spray, which would kill most species. This enables them to spread over large areas of the shore where other plants cannot grow. Although the soil is usually very shallow and poor, they can often flourish in the few pockets of fertile earth that build up in crevices and on rocky cliff ledges.

SALT MARSHES
In cooler regions, the upper shores of sheltered river estuaries are overrun by low-growing plants such as sea lavender and cord grass. These plants are unusual because they can survive being flooded by salt water at high tide. Each plant species has a different tolerance to this, so they grow in well marked zones above midtide level. They form broad, muddy salt marshes, which are important refuges and feeding sites for shorebirds and other animals.

MANGROVES
The tropical equivalent of a salt marsh is a mangrove swamp—a forest of salt-tolerant trees that are specially adapted to grow in tidal mud. They have modified roots that rise above the mud to absorb oxygen from the air. The roots also trap mud suspended in the water, enabling mangroves to spread along coasts. They provide habitats for a variety of animals from baby fish to crocodiles, besides forming natural barriers to storm waves.

SEAGRASS MEADOWS
Seagrasses are the only flowering plants that live underwater. They grow on sandy seabeds in sheltered, shallow water, in tidal estuaries, and coral reef lagoons. They are an important source of food for sea turtles, the strange "sea cows" known as dugongs, and—at low tide—grazing birds such as geese. Seagrass meadows also provide vital refuge for small fish, such as this seahorse, as well as the young of bigger fish that live in deeper water as adults.

# LIFE IN ICY OCEANS

The shores of polar oceans are mostly barren, bare rock, because the sea ice that forms in winter destroys most shore life. Around Antarctica, seals and penguins follow the edge of the sea ice as it expands away from the coast, so they can hunt in open water. This takes them far out into the Southern Ocean. In the north, ice covers most of the Arctic Ocean in winter, so animals congregate around the few remaining patches of open water. But when the ice melts in summer, the cold waters teem with life as plankton multiplies in the almost perpetual daylight.

▲ BARREN BEACHES
Frozen solid in winter, and scoured by moving ice as the tide rises and falls, many of the shores of polar oceans are bare wastes of rock and gravel. But this does not concern animals that feed in the sea, such as these Arctic walruses, which use them to rest and warm up after hunting for shellfish in the cold water. Their pinkish brown skins contrast with the gray of the few animals that are still cold.

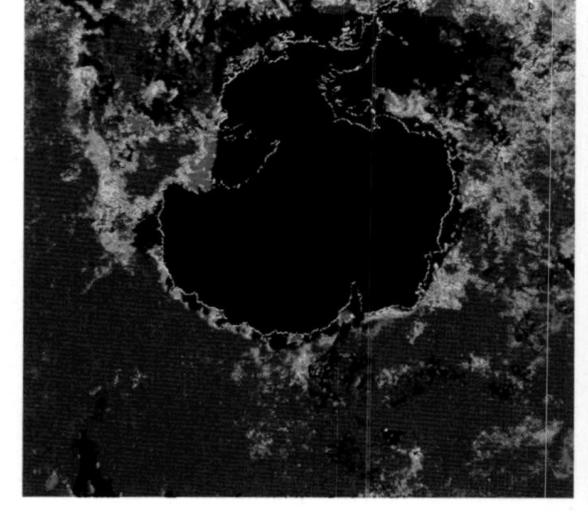

RICH SEAS ►
In shallow polar seas, storms stir up nutrients from the seabed and mix them with the surface water. This enables plankton to multiply rapidly and create a wealth of food when the pack ice breaks up, as shown in red and yellow in this satellite image of Antarctica in summer.

▲ SWARMING KRILL
Around Antarctica, the multiplying phytoplankton is harvested by vast swarms of shrimplike krill that can cover huge areas of ocean. They are the main prey of most of the animals that live on and around Antarctica. These include huge whales that use the sievelike bristles fringing their enormous mouths to strain the krill from the water. Krill also support many penguins, seabirds, and seals.

LEADS AND POLYNAS

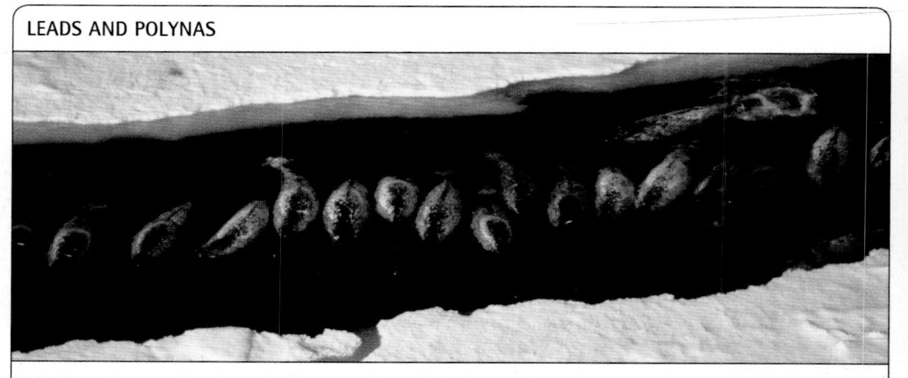

In the winter and spring, the few stretches of the Arctic Ocean that do not freeze over act as magnets for marine mammals like these narwhals. They find all their food in the water, but they must be able to surface to breathe, and this is much more difficult where the ocean surface is frozen. Broad polynas (large areas of open water surrounded by sea ice) and narrower leads (like the one seen here) also attract fish-eating seabirds in spring. Most polynas open up in spring as the pack ice starts melting, but some—such as Northwater between Canada and Greenland—stay open throughout the winter.

**HUNTING UNDER THE ICE ►**
Many seals hunt fish and squid under the ice, surfacing to breathe at the ice edge. But as the Antarctic pack ice expands north in winter, weddell seals stay behind, feeding beneath the pack ice. They breathe through holes that they make in the ice by using their teeth to chip away the ice around existing cracks. Most weddell seals have badly worn teeth as a result, and some die from serious dental infections.

**◄ ICY WATERS**
Salt seawater freezes at 28.8°F (-1.8°C), so it can be colder than the freezing point of fresh water. Animals that live in the water below the pack ice must cope with temperatures that might freeze their bodies. Many polar fish and shellfish survive because they have natural antifreezes in their body fluids. Since food is plentiful on the seabed, these animals can live beneath the ice in large numbers.

**► SEAL COLONIES**
In the Arctic, female seals climb out onto the ice to give birth to their pups. Harp seals form large colonies on unstable pack ice, which cannot support the prowling polar bears that are their main enemies. Harp seals feed their white-coated pups on rich milk for just 12 days before returning to the water.

**◄ BREEDING PENGUINS**
Most Antarctic penguins breed on rocky shores in summer, choosing places where there is no ice to freeze their eggs. Many species like this king penguin breed on the islands fringing the Southern Ocean, which thaw out for longer than the Antarctic continent. It supports its egg on its large webbed feet, covering it with a flap of skin to keep it warm. Uniquely, the closely related emperor penguin uses the same method to breed on sea ice close to Antarctica, incubating its egg thoughout the harsh polar winter.

**◄ SEA BEAR**
The polar bear is a specialized marine predator that lives on the Arctic sea ice. It preys mainly on seals—especially ringed seal pups in spring—and follows the edge of the stable pack ice as it advances and recedes with the seasons. When the pack ice breaks up in summer it is often forced to swim to the land. But here it has trouble finding food, and many polar bears die of starvation. Its future is seriously threatened by the dwindling area of summer sea ice in the Arctic caused by global warming.

# CORAL REEFS AND ATOLLS

The clear waters of tropical oceans contain few of the nutrients that are essential to oceanic life, yet they support one of the richest ecosystems on Earth—tropical coral reefs. Their living wealth is based on a partnership between simple animals called corals and microscopic, plantlike organisms that make food using the energy of sunlight, just like phytoplankton. The growing corals form massive living reefs, populated by a dazzling diversity of animal life.

▲ REEF CORALS
Corals are animals that are closely related to sea anemones. They have the same cylindrical bodies crowned with stinging tentacles for catching small animals. Many live in interconnected colonies, including tropical reef-building corals, which are unique because they have microscopic plantlike zooxanthellae living in their tissues. These are supplied with vital nutrients by their hosts, and in return they use solar energy to make food that the corals need.

BUILDING REEFS ►
Since they need sunlight, reef corals live in clear, shallow water. Their soft bodies are supported by skeletons of limestone, which build up into rocky reefs. These reefs have steep sides facing the open ocean, but often enclose shallow lagoons.

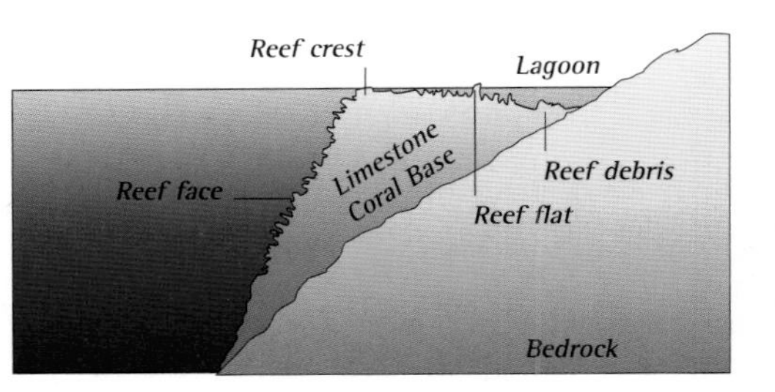


*Lettuce coral*
*Massive star coral*
*Red coralline algae*
*Brain coral*
*Seagrass*
*Sea fan*
*Branched elkhorn coral*
*Flattened star coral*
*Sea whip*

***Lagoon** is dominated by sand and seagrass*

***Reef flat** is sheltered, but the water is often very warm and salty*

***Reef crest** is colonized by red coralline algae that cements coral fragments together*

***Reef face** is exposed to the open ocean, but has the richest diversity of corals*

► REEF ZONES
The reef face is colonized by strong corals that can withstand ocean waves. Broad, flattened types grow in deeper water, while branching corals are common near the top. The reef crest, where waves break, is a mass of coral fragments cemented together with red coralline algae, a type of seaweed. Behind this lies the sheltered reef flat, which often gives way to a sandy lagoon.

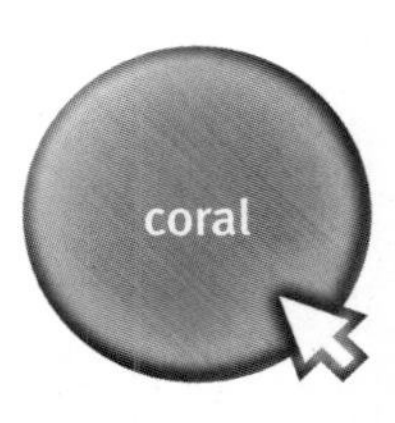

## REEF LIFE

REEF FISH
A huge variety of colorful fish live on the reefs. Some feed on coral or plantlike algae, while others prey on the many animals that live alongside them. Coral reefs support more fish species than any other ocean habitat, each specialized for its own way of life. Yet the total mass of fish is never as great as in the dense fish shoals of more nutrient-rich waters.

SHRIMP
The reefs swarm with shellfish and other invertebrates, including marine snails, colorful sea slugs, sea urchins, and crabs. Cleaner shrimp make a living by picking parasites off the skin, and even gills, of reef fish that queue up for treatment like cars at a busy car wash. Although many of these fish may eat other types of small animals, they never eat the cleaner shrimp.

GIANT CLAM
These enormous mollusks live in crevices in the reef, where they may grow to 5 ft (1.5 m) across. They catch plankton by filter-feeding, but like the reef corals they get most of their energy from sugar made by the zooxanthellae living in their colorful soft tissues. The biggest giant clams are unable to close their shells fully, and cannot grab divers' legs as people once believed.

REEF SHARK
The reefs are patrolled by big predators like this reef shark, which hunt for small fish and other animals. They usually stay in the deeper water outside the reef face, seizing anything that ventures beyond the safety of the coral, but sometimes they swim into the shallow lagoon through gaps in the reef. Many hunt at night, using highly tuned senses to locate their prey in the dark.

### ► CORAL ATOLLS

The tropical Pacific is dotted with volcanic islands that have fringing reefs. When the volcanoes stop erupting, the islands gradually sink under their own weight, but their reefs keep growing upward. They become barrier reefs around shrinking central islands, and finally develop into ring-shaped atolls around roughly circular lagoons.

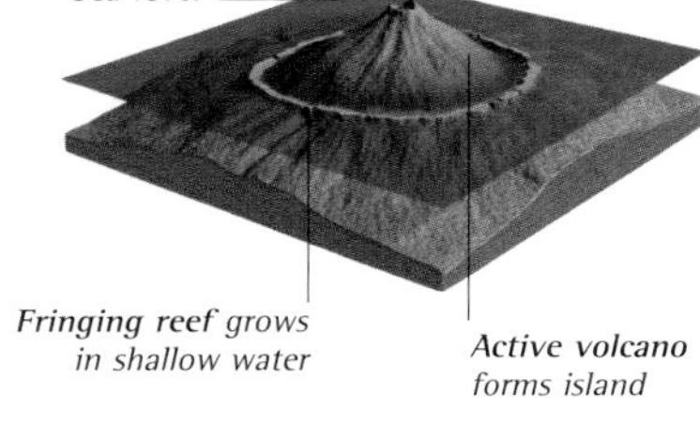


FRINGING REEF

BARRIER REEF

ATOLL

### ◄ LAGOONS AND ISLANDS

The shallow, sun-warmed lagoon waters can reach temperatures of 95°F (35°C) or more. This is too hot for corals, but mobile animals, like these sharks, feed in the water when it is cooler. Low, palm-crowned islands that were built up from coral debris and sand are used as nesting sites by green turtles and frigate birds.

### CROWN-OF-THORNS STARFISH

The crown-of-thorns starfish eats corals, turning its stomach inside out to engulf its prey. It can multiply into hungry swarms that wipe out large areas of coral, leaving dead white coral rock. But these starfish plagues are usually followed by population crashes when the starfish die off, and this gives the coral a chance to recover.

# THE OPEN OCEANS

In deep oceans, the nutrients that fuel plankton growth settle on the ocean floor far below the sunlit zone. This means that there is often very little plankton, especially in deep tropical oceans where the warm surface water rarely mixes with deeper, richer water. In cooler oceans, seasonal storms stir nutrients into the surface waters, allowing marine life to flourish. Yet, even in the tropics, local upwelling can create dense concentrations of ocean life.

▲ CLEAR BLUE WATER
In open tropical oceans, sun-warmed surface water forms a floating layer above deep, cold water containing nutrients. The warm and cold water do not mix and this cuts off the nutrient supply that is vital to life in the sunlit zone, resulting in very little plankton. The water is crystal clear and virtually lifeless.

MIXING ZONES

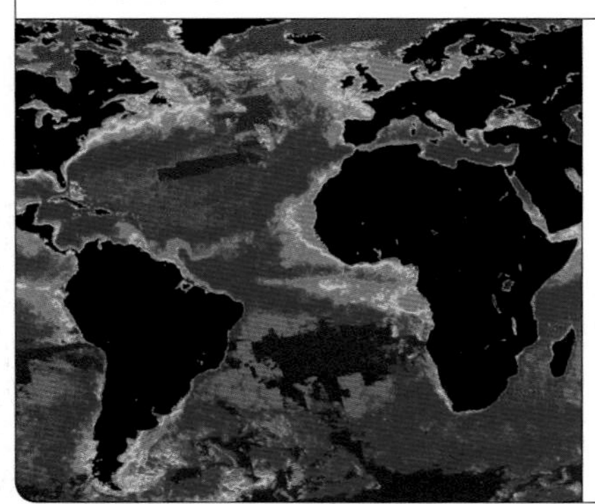

This satellite image of plankton distribution shows the barren zones of tropical oceans in pink and deep blue. They contrast with vivid areas of orange, yellow, and green indicating the dense plankton of cold oceans and upwelling zones. Here, nutrient-rich water is brought to the surface by currents, and in cold oceans by seasonal storms and the sinking of chilled surface water. This causes plankton blooms in cold oceans in the fall and spring.

► NOMADS AND MIGRANTS
Plankton is widely scattered in tropical oceans, and so are the animals that eat it. Many, such as big manta rays and whale sharks, wander over vast areas in search of local concentrations of food. In cold oceans, the plankton blooms of fall and spring encourage more regular migrations. Shoaling fish, dolphins, and giants like this humpback whale arrive at the same times each year to make the most of the seasonal riches and then leave when the food runs out.

◄ HIGH-SPEED HUNTERS
The predators that roam the open ocean are equipped for covering long distances as quickly as possible. They include tuna that hunt in packs and solitary hunters like oceanic sharks and this blue marlin. They are streamlined, powerful animals, and some are able to swim at speeds of well over 50 mph (80 kph).

▲ BAITBALLS
Small, plankton-feeding fish travel in shoals that bunch together in dense "baitballs" when they are attacked by bigger fish, spinning and swirling to confuse their enemies. But the commotion—and the scent of blood from casualties—often attracts more predators that join the attack in a feeding frenzy.

▼ AIRBORNE FISH
Tropical flyingfish have extended fins that act as wings, enabling them to leap clear of the water and glide through the air if they are attacked. This is a good way of escaping predatory fish such as tuna, but airborne flyingfish are often targeted by oceanic frigate birds that swoop down to seize them in their bills.

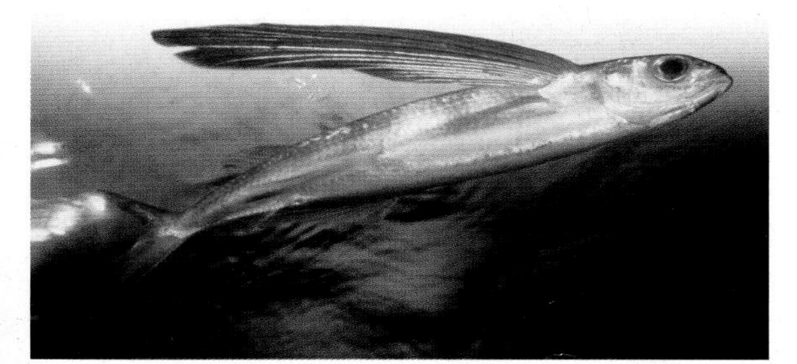

► SEAMOUNT HOTSPOTS
The floor of the Pacific is dotted with extinct submarine volcanoes called seamounts. These can cause local upwelling zones as ocean currents push cold, nutrient-rich water up their slopes in eddies that swirl toward the surface. The nutrients promote the growth of plankton, which provides food for local concentrations of fish. These attract bigger fish and powerful predators such as sharks, creating wildlife hotspots in tropical deep oceans where marine life can be scarce.

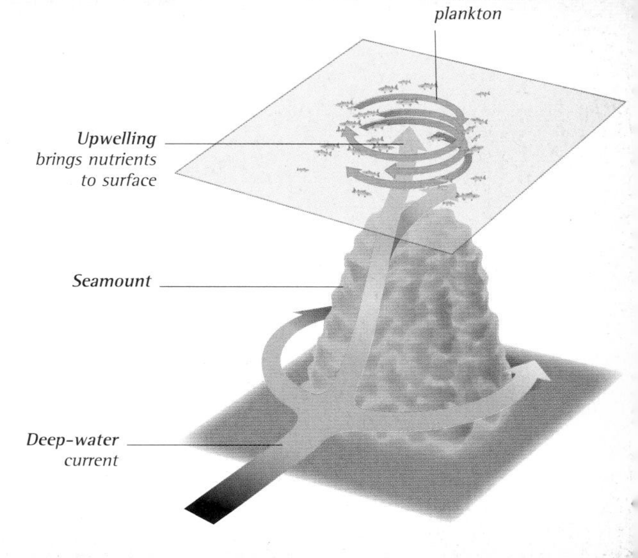

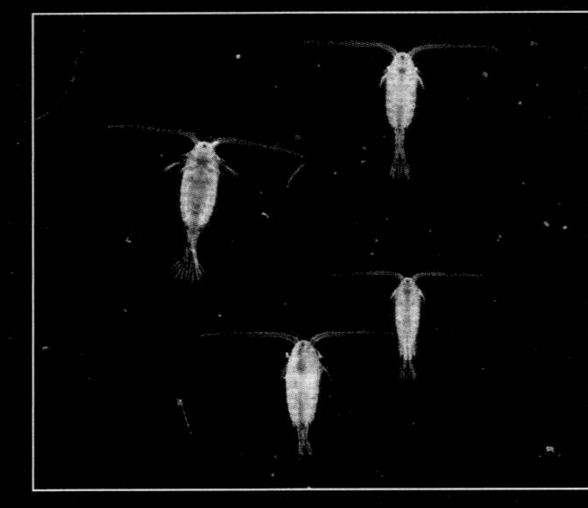

▲ VERTICAL MIGRATIONS
Zooplankton such as these copepods graze on phytoplankton near the surface at night, but at dawn they retreat to the twilight zone up to 3,300 ft (1,000 m) below, to avoid shoals of hungry fish. They migrate upward again in the evening—a long journey for such tiny creatures.

# THE OCEAN DEPTHS

In the dark waters beneath the sunlit zone, the primary food source is dead material that drifts down from above. This has low food value compared to the living phytoplankton near the surface, so the zooplankton that live in the twilight zone by day migrate toward the surface at night to feed. Fish that eat the zooplankton migrate upward with them, and are targeted from below by bigger predators. Many of these fish glow in the dark, and have huge mouths and long teeth for seizing scarce prey. By contrast, most of the animals that live on the deep ocean floor feed on dead animals and other debris.

*Silvery body* reflects light to confuse enemies

*Bulging eyes* look upward to pick out prey

ocean depths

*Light organs* produce camouflaging blue glow

◄ HATCHETFISH
The zooplankton that live in the twilight zone by day are hunted by hatchetfish. These have upward-facing eyes that enable them to see their prey against the dim blue light filtering down from the surface. Their bellies are studded with luminous organs that match the blue glow, concealing their own silhouettes from bigger hunters.

► WEIRD GLOW
Thousands of deep-water animals like this squid glow in the dark. They have light organs called photophores, which use a chemical reaction to generate light without heat. The animals use the light to confuse their enemies, to signal to one another in the gloom, and to lure or spotlight their prey.

*Glowing organs* flash messages in the dark

◄ MONSTERS OF THE DEEP
Prey is so scarce in the depths that hunters must be able to eat anything they run into. The monstrous-looking gulper eel can swallow animals as big as itself, thanks to its enormous mouth and an elastic stomach that can stretch like a balloon.

NIGHTMARE HUNTERS ►
Many deep-ocean predators like this fangtooth have gaping mouths and long teeth to snare their prey. Yet most of these nightmare hunters are fairly small, since prey is too scarce to support big-bodied predators.

***Broad mouth** has teeth like a trap*

▲ SUPERSENSES
Angler fish that live in the deep ocean use luminous lures to entice prey within range of their wickedly sharp teeth. Some of these fish also bristle with hairlike sensory rays, which detect slight movements in the darkness and alert them to prey.

***Hairlike rays** act as movement sensors*

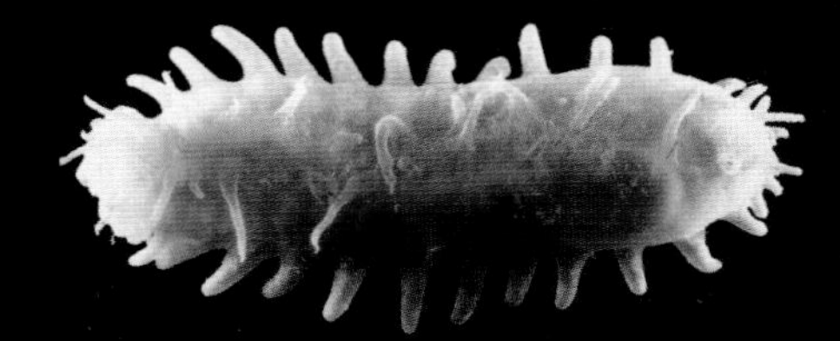

◄ SCAVENGERS OF THE DEEP
Dead animals that drift down from above are attacked by a variety of scavengers, including deep-water crustaceans such as amphipods and shrimps, rat-tail fish, and the slimy, eel-like hagfish shown here. Yet many carcasses take so long to sink through the deep, dark water that they are eaten before they reach the bottom.

MUD PROCESSORS ▲
The abyssal plains are populated by animals such as this sea cucumber, or holothurian, which suck up the sediments, swallow them, and digest any food. The mud and ooze are full of buried crustaceans, worms, and microbes, which feed beneath the surface of the ocean floor. Together, they gather every grain of food that reaches the bottom of the ocean.

# HYDROTHERMAL VENTS

Volcanic midocean ridges are peppered with submarine geysers that erupt hot water full of dissolved chemicals. These hydrothermal vents support dense communities of animals that grow much faster, and bigger, than most deep ocean life. This is because they do not depend on the little food that drifts down from the surface. They have their own food supply, created by using the chemical energy of the vents themselves. This ecosystem is one of the few on Earth that does not rely on sunlight.

◄ **CHEMICAL CLOUDS**
The hot water that pours from hydrothermal vents contains dissolved metal sulfides that turn into solid, sooty particles when they mix with cold ocean water. The particles can make the water look like black smoke, so the vents are often called black smokers. Some of the chemicals are lethal to most marine life, but the organisms that live around black smokers not only survive them, but also thrive on them.

**MAKING FOOD**

The rocks around hydrothermal vents are covered with dense white mats of microscopic bacteria. These are able to absorb the normally toxic hydrogen sulfide in the hot vent water and combine it with oxygen in a chemical reaction that produces energy. They use the energy to make sugar from water and dissolved carbon dioxide, in a process called chemosynthesis. This is like photosynthesis, but it does not need light. It is likely that some of the earliest forms of life on Earth made food in the same way.

**POMPEII WORMS** ►
The water that gushes from hydrothermal vents can be astonishingly hot, reaching 850°F (450°C) or more. Yet some animals can live surprisingly close to the superheated water. The 4 in (10 cm) long Pompeii worm lives on the chimneys that build up around vents, with its head in water at a temperature of about 70°F (20°C), but its tail in water heated to 160°F (70°C) or more. This would kill any other animal.

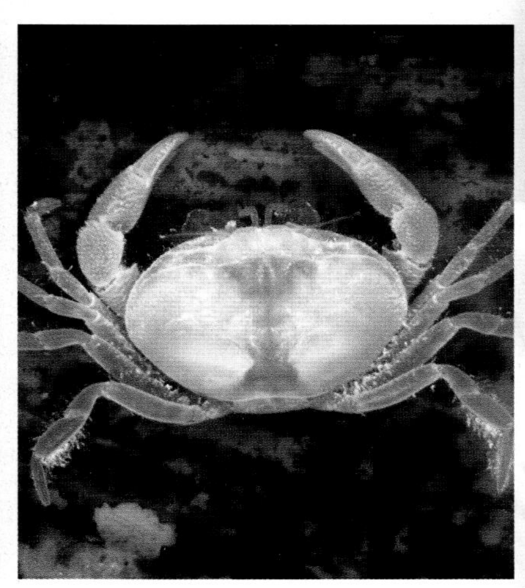

▲ CRABS

The mats of bacteria around Pacific vents are grazed by armies of blind white crabs, and similar swarms of shrimp feed on the bacterial mats around Atlantic vents. Big colonies of mussels and clams also rely on the bacteria for food, but allow it to grow inside their shells, on their gills. Having such a reliable food source enables them to grow fast, and turn into giants with shells up to 10 in (25 cm) long.

GIANT TUBEWORMS ►

The most spectacular vent animals are giant tubeworms up to 6 ft (2 m) long, with bright red gill plumes. They live in clumps around the vents, where they absorb the chemically rich water and supply it to colonies of bacteria living inside their bodies. The bacteria make food that the worms can use to build their tissues, just like the organisms that live in partnership with tropical reef corals. This enables the worms to grow much faster than most deep-sea life.

▲ METHANE SEEPS

Similar living communities of bacteria have been found around places where methane (natural gas) is seeping from the ocean floor. The high pressure at depth makes the methane freeze into a form of ice. Bacteria process this and use it to make food that supports ice worms and other animals.

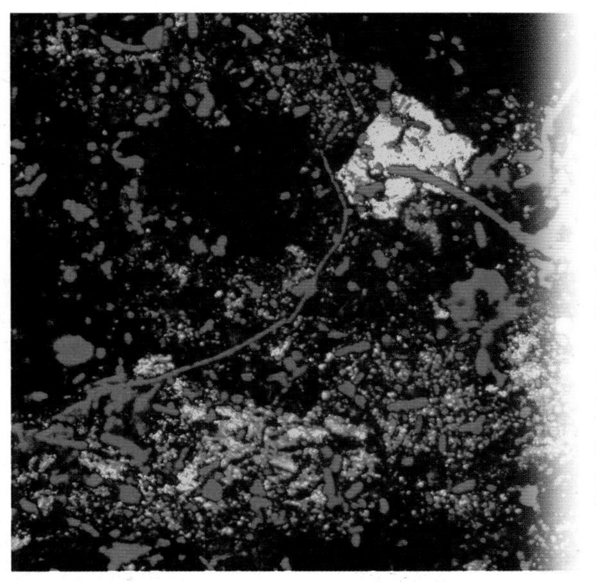

◄ LIVING IN THE ROCK

Bacteria that make food by chemosynthesis have been found living beneath the ocean floor, deep in the sediments, and between layers of solid sedimentary rock. Shown here in red, they survive by turning hydrogen and carbon dioxide into methane, producing energy to make their food. Their ability to live in this extreme environment suggests how life may have started on Earth. These organisms may also be able to live in even more extreme conditions—such as beneath the surface of Mars.

# MINERALS FROM THE SEA

For centuries, people have been using the oceans as a source of salt, and also collecting other materials ranging from beach sand to pearls. But the mineral resources of the seafloor were almost unknown until quite recently, when the technology needed to exploit them was developed. The most important of these resources are oil and natural gas, tapped from reserves buried deep in the rocks of the continental shelves. The seas are also a major source of gravel and sand, and even diamonds. But many oceanic minerals are too difficult and expensive to harvest, especially those found on the deep ocean floor.

▲ SEA SALT
The most abundant mineral in ocean water is sodium chloride, or common salt. It is extracted by evaporating seawater in shallow, sunlit salt pans. This simple process has been used for thousands of years, and it still meets roughly a third of the world's need for salt.

FRESH WATER ►
Some countries use the sea as a source of water for drinking purposes and crop irrigation, but the salty seawater has to be pumped through a desalination plant to remove the salt. It is an expensive process that uses a lot of energy, so it is mainly used in the rich desert states, especially in the Middle East. The desalination plant shown here is in Kuwait, on the desert shores of the Persian Gulf, and nearly a quarter of the world's desalinated water is produced in neighbouring Saudi Arabia.

### OIL AND GAS

The thick sediments covering many seafloors hold large reserves of oil and gas, formed from the decomposed remains of marine organisms. Initially, only the reserves beneath shallow continental shelves were exploited, but offshore platforms, like the one shown below, now work in water up to 10,000 ft (3,000 m) deep. They may drill 16,500 ft (5,000 m) or more below the seabed.

◄ AGGREGATES
Vast amounts of gravel and sand are dredged from the seafloor to feed the construction industry. Simple cranes mounted on barges are used in shallow water, as here, but special dredging ships work in deeper water. The quartz sand found on many beaches is also used for making glass.

◄ MANGANESE NODULES
Several parts of the deep ocean floor are covered with potato-sized nodules containing valuable elements such as manganese, cobalt, and titanium. But since they lie more than 13,000 ft (4,000 m) below the surface, harvesting them would cost more than they are worth.

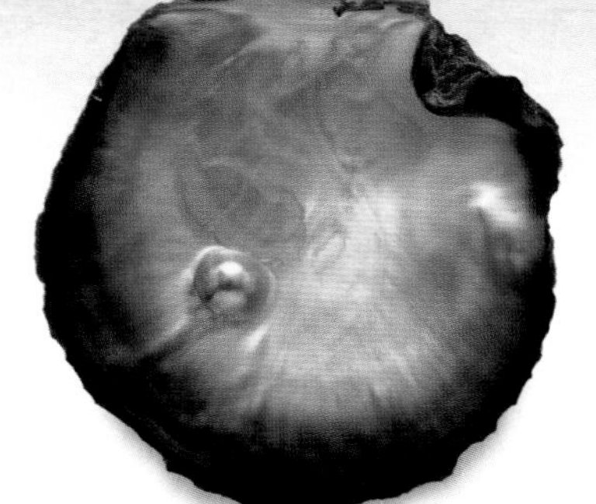

◄ PEARLS AND DIAMONDS
The natural pearls formed within oyster shells have been gathered by pearl divers for centuries. Even more valuable, however, are the gemstones found on the barren Atlantic shores of southwest Africa, where the coastal sands contain diamonds carried off the continent by ancient rivers.

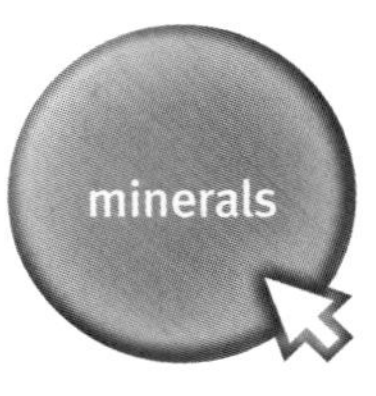


◄ METALS AND METHANE
The hydrothermal vents on mid-ocean ridges erupt hot water that is rich in dissolved metals. It is possible that these could be harvested, although they lie a long way beneath the ocean surface. There are also extensive reserves of frozen methane beneath the ocean floors, which could be tapped for natural gas. This might be hazardous, however, because the accidental release of methane on a large scale could cause catastrophic climate change.

# ENERGY FROM THE OCEANS

The ocean is always on the move. Storm waves can unleash enough energy to smash concrete, and tides and currents shift vast quantities of water around the globe. The oceans are swept by some of the most powerful winds on Earth. All these forces could be used to generate electricity in ways that do not pollute the environment. For decades we have relied on energy produced by burning coal, oil, and gas, which release gases that cause climate change. As these old technologies are phased out, the oceans will become a major source of energy.

◄ LOST ARTS
Before coal power was widely adopted in the late 18th century, all energy was renewable. Even iron was produced using water power and charcoal made from renewable lumber. Ships were driven by the wind, and tide-powered mills were common. We need to reinvent these technologies for a new age.

► WAVE ENERGY
Waves are an obvious source of energy, but it is difficult to turn them into reliable power. This plant in Scotland converts the force of the waves into air pressure, which drives two turbines connected to electricity generators. The system works well, but only because the site is exposed to big waves throughout the year.

▲ WIND POWER
The wind is already being used to generate electricity on a massive scale, using wind turbines. Many of these are situated on land, but offshore turbines like these work better because the winds at sea are stronger and more dependable. The largest offshore wind farm in the world has been built in Denmark, where wind power provides a fifth of the country's electricity.

TIDAL BARRAGES ►
The tide can be harnessed by building a barrage across a river estuary, which lets the water flood in freely, then releasing it through turbines that drive electricity generators. This tidal power plant in St. Malo in France has been running since 1967. Bigger programs are planned, but they could seriously damage local marine habitats.

▲ OCEAN CURRENTS
The relentless power of ocean currents has never been used to generate electricity, but there are plans to exploit the energy of the Gulf Stream where it flows between Florida and the Bahamas. This artist's impression shows how it might be done, using a series of submerged, tethered turbines to drive the generators. This could produce as much electricity as a nuclear power plant.

▲ REINVENTING THE SAIL
Provided they are used to carry heavy cargo, ships are an extremely efficient form of transportation. Even normal cargo ships burn a lot less fuel than air freight, but their efficiency could be increased by using the wind as a power source. One design uses fiberglass aerofoils that work like sails, while another uses a giant inflatable kite.

# FISHING AND MARICULTURE

People have been fishing in coastal waters since prehistoric times, and many ancient fishing techniques are still used today. But commercial fishing has now become a major industry, with fleets of ships equipped with advanced technology for finding, catching, and processing fish. Many species of fish are also reared in captivity, in various forms of mariculture such as fish farms and shrimp pools.

▲ COASTAL FISHING
Most coastal communities practice some form of fishing to supply the nearby markets. These simple techniques yield just enough fish to meet the local demand. Since they are rarely intensive enough to threaten fish populations, the fishermen never run out of fish to catch. They are not very profitable, but they are sustainable—provided the same waters are not used for industrial fishing as well.

◄ OCEANIC FLEETS
Most of the fish that are eaten worldwide are caught by fleets of big fishing boats that stay at sea for months. Their catch is processed and refrigerated on board, or on factory ships. Such fishing fleets venture as far as the Southern Ocean, although most of the fishing takes place in the north Atlantic and north Pacific Oceans, and in the rich seas off Chile and Peru.

NETS AND LINES ►
The simple drift nets once used for sea fishing have given way to purse seine nets that surround and trap entire shoals, and big trawl nets that scoop up huge numbers of bottom-feeding fish such as cod. Tuna are often caught on longlines with up to 10,000 baited hooks, trailing up to 75 miles (120 km) behind the ship.

▲ SHRIMP POOLS
The Far East has a long tradition of mariculture, and for centuries, fish and other marine animals such as tiger shrimp have been raised in tidal pools dug for the purpose on low-lying coasts. Unlike normal fishing this is a form of farming rather than hunting, so it has no direct effect on the wild stocks. But it can have other environmental impacts, especially when tidal mangroves are cleared to make way for the pools. This destroys habitats that are a vital refuge for the young of many valuable sea fish, and also makes local communities more vulnerable to oceanic storms.

▲ MUSSEL BEDS
Mussels and oysters are ideal for farming, because they naturally attach themselves to rocks and other hard surfaces and do not bury themselves in the sand or mud. These mussels are being grown on ropes twisted around wooden posts on the Atlantic coast of France, where they are submerged by the tide twice a day.

fishing

## SATELLITES AND FISHFINDERS

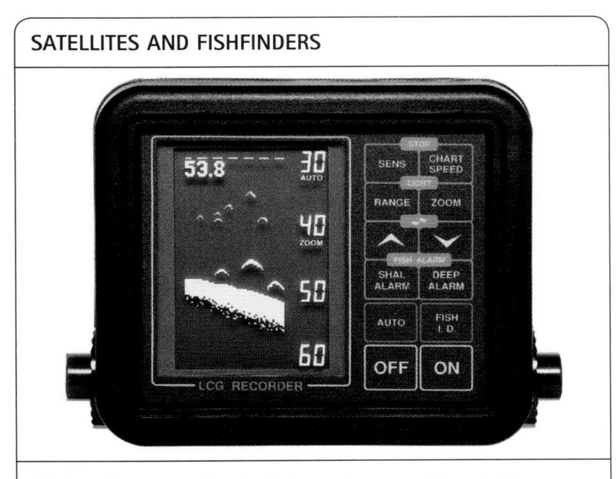


Fishing skippers are aided in their search by a variety of high-technology equipment. Many have access to satellite imagery that shows where dense plankton swarms are likely to attract fish. They also use refined echo-sounders called fishfinders that use sound pulses to detect fish in the water below the ship. These can penetrate as deep as the twilight zone, and reveal fish shoals as distinctive traces on the screen called "fish arches." Several of these can be seen on the fishfinder screen shown above, along with a broad band of white that indicates the position of the seabed.

► SALMON CAGES
Most sea fish do not do well if they are kept in confined spaces, but salmon are an exception. They can be raised in submerged cages like these, in clear, cool tidal waters that sweep through the cages and keep the fish healthy. They have to be fed, however, and the uneaten food and fish waste can upset the local balance of nature. Despite this, the salmon farming industry is very successful, and has reduced fishing pressure on wild salmon.

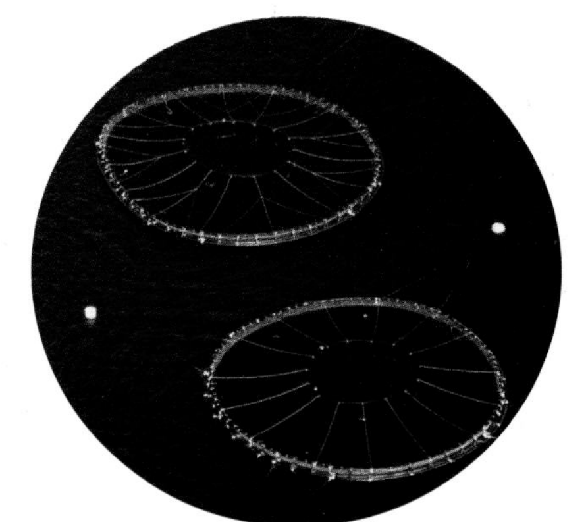

► SEAWEED FARMS
Seaweed is a surprisingly valuable material, since it is used as a thickening agent in a wide range of products, including toothpaste and ice cream. It is also cooked and eaten in many areas, especially in China and other countries in the Far East. A lot is gathered from the wild, but in the Indo-Pacific region seaweed farming is a flourishing industry, with an annual production that exceeds the output of all other forms of mariculture put together. Here, a seaweed farmer tends her crop in the shallow waters off the coast of Zanzibar, east Africa.

# OVERFISHING AND BYCATCH

Modern commercial fishing is so intense that many fish are becoming rare. Bigger ships, better nets, and new technology for locating fish are no longer resulting in larger catches, and the global fish catch actually fell by 13 percent between 1994 and 2003. The variety of fish found along coasts has also been badly affected. Other marine wildlife is threatened by the accidental bycatch of turtles, seabirds, dolphins, and seals, as well as the wrong kind of fish. Overfishing is threatening to drive some species, such as albatrosses, to global extinction.

WORLD DEMAND

The massive increase in the world's human population is putting extreme pressure on some natural resources, including sea fish. The annual global fish catch now stands at more than 83 million tons (75 million metric tons). Some is sold whole in markets like this, but most is frozen or canned. Fish populations are collapsing, and if the current trend continues, most of the world's fish stocks will be wiped out by 2050.

◄ NETTING SHOALS
Modern fish-location techniques and purse seine nets make it possible to catch entire shoals of fish. This may seem rather like netting a football crowd, but it is more like destroying an isolated tribe with its own genetic identity. It reduces the genetic variety of the species, making it more vulnerable to extinction.

▲ NO TIME TO BREED
Some fish like these orange roughy do not breed until they are several years old, and even then they breed slowly. They cannot make up for losses caused by intensive fishing, so they go into steep decline. Before long they may be virtually extinct.

## FISH UNDER THREAT

COD
This favorite target of the fishing industry has been virtually fished out from the two main fisheries—the North Sea and the Grand Banks. A female produces millions of eggs when she spawns, but many never get the chance.

TUNA
As oceanic predators, tuna are much rarer than the fish that they prey upon. Pulling them out of the sea to be canned in huge numbers is destroying their small populations, and some species are now in serious danger.

SHARKS
Vast number of sharks are caught so their fins can be cut off for sharks' fin soup. They are then dumped back in the water—often while still alive. This cruel trade is making these slow breeders a rare species.

◄ WHALING
We know how destructive overfishing can be, considering the fate of the world's whales. By the time whaling was virtually banned in 1986, intensive hunting had almost wiped out species like the giant blue whale. Even today, it is very rare because the few survivors breed slowly.

◄ DOLPHIN BYCATCH
All kinds of marine animals are accidentally caught by fishing fleets. Many are fish of the wrong type, while others are air-breathing animals that get trapped in fishing nets and drown. Dolphins often follow tuna shoals, and if the tuna are netted, the dolphins may be caught, too. Despite various systems designed to prevent this, many thousands of dolphins still die every year.

◄ LONGLINING FOR SEABIRDS
Some fish are caught on lines with thousands of baited hooks. As each line streams from the boat into the water, birds like this gannet swoop down to seize the bait. They get hooked, dragged under, and drowned. Up to 100,000 albatrosses die like this each year. Many people are trying to stop the slaughter before most of the 21 species of albatrosses become extinct.

# OCEAN TRADE AND TOURISM

Oceans have always been important trading routes. Ships still provide one of the most efficient ways of transporting heavy materials such as oil over long distances, while container ships carry all kinds of goods, from frozen food to cars and computers. The sea is also an important element of the tourist trade, because most of the places that tourists visit are beach resorts. Many people even enjoy traveling by sea, either on big cruise ships or on their own small yachts, pitting their sailing skills against the power of the ocean.

▲ BULK CARRIERS AND CONTAINERS
Ships are the only economic means of carrying heavy materials like oil and sand across the oceans, and container ships like this one can carry a colossal amount of cargo. This is because a ship and its load are supported by the water, and the amount of fuel needed to propel it does not increase in proportion with the weight of its payload. By contrast, an aircraft uses a huge quantity of fuel simply staying airborne, and this increases with every extra pound of freight that it carries.

▲ CANAL LINKS
Oceanic trading became safer and quicker when the Suez Canal in Egypt and the Panama Canal in Central America were built in the 19th and early 20th centuries, respectively. By cutting through the narrow necks of land linking the great continents, the canals enabled ships to trade between the Indian, Atlantic, and Pacific Oceans without making long, dangerous voyages around the stormy southern capes of Africa and South America.

◄ BUSY PORTS
Most coastal cities were built using the wealth created by the ocean trade. Some still have busy ports, but today many ships dock at terminals that are situated far from city centers. These facilities are often especially designed for handling specific cargo, like these containers.

◄ CRUISE SHIPS
Ocean liners were once the only way for people to travel between continents. Today, airlines have made global travel much quicker, but the ships have been reinvented as giant floating hotels, taking tourists on cruises to exotic destinations such as Tahiti and Antarctica. However, ships use a huge amount of fuel per passenger, because unlike bulk freight, people do not weigh much compared to the ship itself.

SAILING TO ADVENTURE

Yachting is a major leisure activity, with many people owning their own boats. It gives them an opportunity to enjoy the beauty of the sea, and a chance to rely on their own skills in an age when our urban lives offer few real challenges.

▲ COASTAL RESORTS
Millions of people flock to coastal resorts each year to spend time on the beach and enjoy the sea. Since the expansion of air travel, tourism has become a major industry on many once-remote islands, such as Mauritius in the Indian Ocean, seen here. The income of such islands now relies heavily on tourism, but developments designed to attract tourists often cause environmental problems.

◄ EXPLORING THE SEA
Since its invention in the 1940s, scuba diving has become an increasingly popular way of exploring the undersea world. The coral reefs of the Red Sea, Maldives, Micronesia, and Australia are big attractions for divers, and small coral islands such as the Maldives rely on divers for much of their tourist income. Other coastal resorts offer people the chance to dive with dolphins or whales, or even experience thrilling encounters with great white sharks.

# HABITAT DESTRUCTION

The oceans are vast, and it once seemed that nothing we did could affect them. People thought that the oceans could absorb anything we dumped in them, from raw sewage to nuclear waste, and that any damage caused by our activities would be quickly healed by the richness of oceanic life. But a combination of overfishing, pollution, and coastal development is destroying many oceanic habitats and killing their wildlife. In some parts of the oceans, the damage is so severe that it may be irreversible, because the wildlife that once flourished there has been wiped out.

◄ RED TIDE
A huge quantity of untreated sewage is pumped into the oceans. This can contain dangerous microbes, and may overstimulate the growth of plankton to create a toxic red tide. When the dense cloud of plankton dies, its decay uses up all the oxygen in the water, killing marine life.

## POLLUTING POISONS

OIL
This is regularly dumped at sea by ships, spilled by wrecked oil tankers, or leaked from damaged oil rigs. It smothers beaches, destroys coastal habitats, and poisons marine life. Oiled seabirds, for example, may survive for long enough to be cleaned up, then die from the toxic effects of the oil they have swallowed.

HEAVY METALS
Metals such as mercury and lead are naturally found in the sea, but in tiny amounts. Industrial waste pumped into the ocean can contain much higher concentrations that are poisonous to sea life. Coastal communities have also suffered heavy metal poisoning by eating contaminated seafood.

PESTICIDES
Chemicals used to kill crop pests are just as effective at killing ocean life when rivers carry the pesticides into the sea. Many of these poisons take a long time to decay, and all kinds of sea creatures from fish to polar bears have been found with high levels of poison in their bodies. This may make them ill, and may even kill them.

► DEADLY GARBAGE
Vast amounts of waste plastic find their way into the oceans, and stay there since plastic does not decay like other forms of garbage. It traps animals like this seal, which has a plastic packing band cutting deep into its flesh. Giant leatherback turtles have been found with their stomachs full of plastic bags, which they swallow because they look like their main prey, jellyfish. Other animals are killed by discarded fishing nets, which keep trapping marine life for years after they have been thrown overboard.

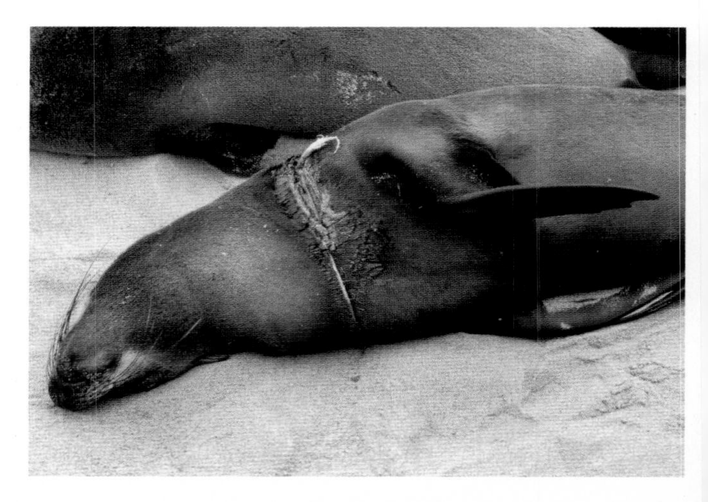

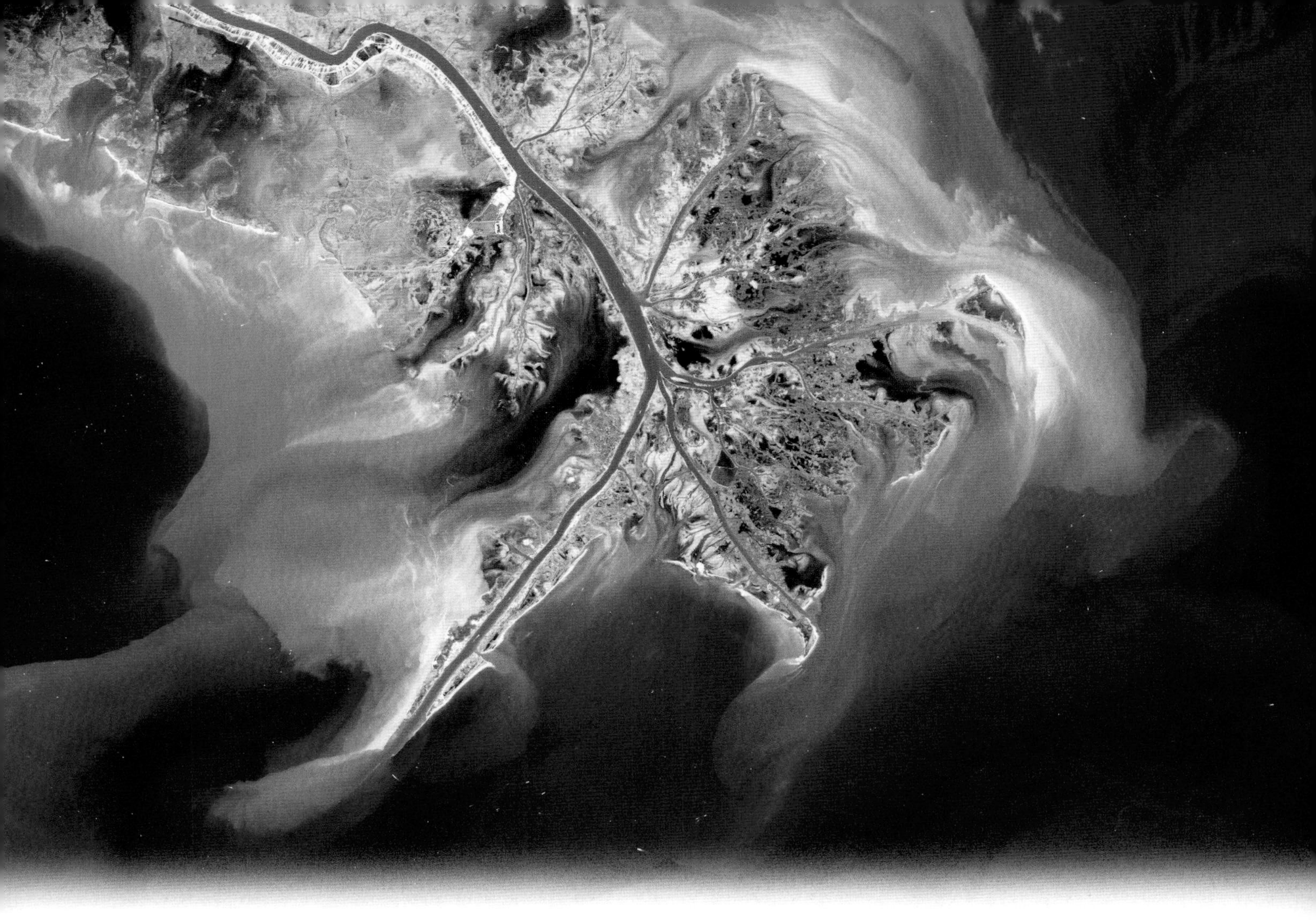

▲ DEAD ZONES
Many rivers are so contaminated with toxins that they have created underwater dead zones where they drain into the sea. One of the biggest lies off the Mississippi Delta in the Gulf of Mexico. Created by the poisoned sediments, seen swirling into the sea in this aerial view, the dead zone covers 8,500 sq miles (22,000 sq km).

COASTAL DESTRUCTION ►
Tourist developments have caused massive destruction of coastal habitats, especially in the tropics. Coastal mangroves have been swept away, exposing coasts to tropical storms. Soil carried off deforested shores by heavy rain also pollutes the sea, smothering nearby coral reefs and seagrass beds.

◄ WRECKED REEFS
Many tropical coral reefs like this one have been damaged by divers and the anchors of dive boats and leisure craft. They also suffer from pollution released by badly planned coastal developments. In Indonesia, valuable reef fish are illegally stunned with cyanide, a deadly poison, so they can be collected for the pet trade—even though the poison soon kills them.

# CLIMATE CHANGE

The greatest threat to the oceans and coastal communities is climate change. Global warming is melting polar ice, raising sea levels, and making violent oceanic storms more common. Oceans are getting warmer, while carbon dioxide pollution is making the water more acidic. This is destroying coral reefs, and could drive a lot of marine life into extinction. Ocean currents are getting disrupted, and if warmer waters trigger melting of the frozen methane that lies beneath the seabed, the effects could be catastrophic.

▲ THE GREENHOUSE EFFECT
The planet is kept warm by an atmospheric blanket of greenhouse gases that retain some of the heat radiated from its sun-warmed surface. One of the most important of these is carbon dioxide, which can be created by burning coal, oil, and gas. Massive use of these fuels has added more carbon dioxide to the air, increasing the greenhouse effect and causing global warming.

▲ MELTING ICE
Rising temperatures are melting the ice sheets of Antarctica and Greenland. Meltwater streaming off the land is causing a rise in sea level, and making polar oceans less salty. The summer sea ice in the Arctic has also shrunk to the smallest area ever recorded. This threatens Arctic wildlife such as the polar bear, which lives on the ice. If the sea ice disappears, the polar bear could vanish, too.

▲ RISING SEA LEVELS
Water added by melting ice threatens to make average sea levels rise by up to 3 ft (1 meter) over the next century, and possibly more. The effect of this will be exaggerated in many regions that are exposed to large tides and storm surges. Coastal cities such as Shanghai in China could be flooded, low-lying lands such as Bangladesh will be swamped, and several island nations will virtually disappear.

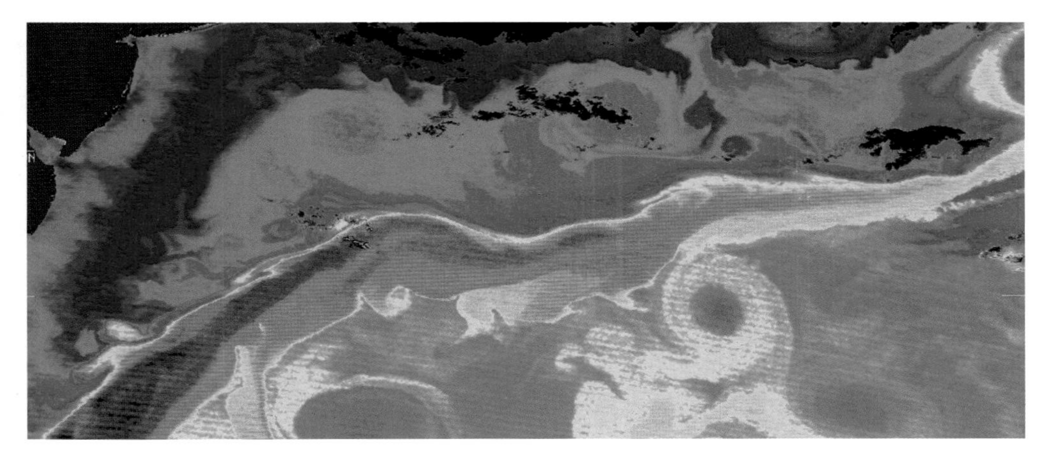

◄ OCEAN CURRENT DISRUPTION

Fresh meltwater draining off melting continental ice sheets is diluting the water of nearby oceans, making it less salty, less dense, and less likely to sink. This is weakening the sinking currents in the north Atlantic Ocean that help drive the warm Gulf Stream current, seen in red in this satellite image. If the Gulf Stream is disrupted, it will seriously affect the climate of northern Europe, and possibly the world.

CORAL BLEACHING ►
Tropical reef corals rely on tiny organisms living in their tissues to provide them with food. These organisms cannot tolerate very warm water. It makes them leave the coral, which then turns white and may die. This coral bleaching damaged a quarter of the world's coral in 1998, and it could become an annual event, gradually destroying one of the world's richest habitats.

▲ STORM WARNING
Destructive hurricanes are fueled by the evaporation of warm ocean water. The warmer the oceans, the more fuel these storms have available, so warmer oceans may cause more storms. These could be more violent where ocean temperatures are highest, and they may also be more widespread. It may be significant that 2005 was the worst Atlantic hurricane season on record.

◄ METHANE THREAT
Carbon dioxide is not the only greenhouse gas causing climate change. It is also caused by methane gas, which is released by many natural processes. There are vast reserves of frozen methane buried in the sediments of the ocean floor. If rising ocean temperatures allow these to melt, they could bubble up through the water and into the atmosphere, dramatically accelerating global warming.

ACID OCEANS

A lot of the carbon dioxide that we have added to the atmosphere has dissolved in the oceans, but has made their waters more acidic. This acid attacks the chalky shells of crustaceans and mollusks such as crabs and clams, and destroys the limestone skeletons of corals. If the problem worsens it could kill off coral reefs worldwide, and cause mass extinction of oceanic shelled animals.

# MARINE CONSERVATION

We cherish the beauty and diversity of life in the oceans, but the future of humanity may also depend on their health. People need to eat, so if the fish stocks that supply up to 20 percent of the world's protein-rich food disappear, then many people may starve. If we allow marine ecosystems to collapse, we have no way of knowing how this might affect life elsewhere. Marine conservation is essential if we are to prevent such destruction. It might not deal with the major challenge of climate change, but if it helps keep the oceans healthy, the oceans may keep the planet healthy, too.

◄ QUOTAS AND TREATIES
Many fisheries are now controlled by international treaties, with each boat having a catch quota that it cannot exceed. Some boats like these in Newfoundland, in Canada, have stopped working altogether, causing hardship for the local people. Yet this is better than the complete destruction of the fish that this industry relies on. Eventually, such treaties should allow fish stocks to recover, but this may take a long time.

MARINE RESERVES ►
In some places, sea areas have been set aside as marine reserves. Fishing and other damaging activities are prohibited, allowing their wildlife to flourish, multiply, and spread into nearby waters. This can dramatically improve both the variety and number of fish, so "no fishing" zones may make fishing in neighboring areas easier and more profitable.

## IMPROVED TECHNOLOGY

For decades, people have been using better equipment to catch more fish. Improved technology can also help with conservation, by making sure that only the target species are caught. The baited longlines that hook albatrosses, for example, can be equipped with bird-scarers like these, or streamed from the boats underwater so the birds cannot see the bait. Specially designed fishing nets may enable dolphins to escape entanglement and drowning. The problem, however, is not designing the equipment, but getting people to use it when they are out of sight of land.

◄ PLANNING LAWS
Many coastal developments are poorly planned. Villas and hotels are built all along the coasts of areas that attract tourists, often destroying the beautiful landscapes that the tourists come to see. Many buildings have no proper drainage, so they cause serious water pollution. Only strict planning laws can stop such destruction.

► POLLUTION CONTROL
A lot of the sewage pumped out to sea is untreated. In some regions, the waste from cities and tourist resorts has destroyed much of the marine wildlife. Effective sewage treatment is a vital part of marine conservation, and so is controlling the pollution of river water. Even clearing the garbage off beaches helps reduce the threat to sea life.

◄ ECOTOURISM
Many regions with spectacular ocean life now use it to attract rich tourists. Ventures such as this whale-watching trip are only possible if the whales are there to be seen. So it pays the local people to conserve their seas by preventing marine pollution and overfishing.

CARBON CUTBACK ►
Aside from giving money and support, most people can do little to help with marine conservation. However, the most important threat of all, global climate change, is something that everyone can help tackle. By simply using less of the energy generated by burning fossil fuels, we can all reduce carbon dioxide emissions and contribute to the future of the oceans, and all life on Earth.

# TIMELINE

**c.1500BCE** Polynesians start to colonize most of the islands of the Pacific Ocean, crossing it in large, double-hulled sailing canoes. They reach Hawaii and New Zealand by 1000 CE.

**c.985CE** Viking mariners reach the coast of Newfoundland in North America after being driven southwest by a storm while sailing to Greenland from Iceland.

**1405–33** Chinese admiral Zheng He explores the Indian Ocean with his fleet.

**1492** Genoese merchant Christopher Columbus uses the trade winds to cross the Atlantic Ocean in search of a sea route to China, but discovers the West Indies instead.

**1519–21** Portuguese navigator Ferdinand Magellan is sent by Spain to find a sea route to the East Indies via the Pacific. After he is killed in the Philippines his crew sails home across the Indian Ocean, and completes the first voyage around the world.

**1735** British physicist George Hadley explains how the Earth's rotation affects the oceanic trade winds. His name is given to the Hadley cells, which are part of the pattern of global air circulation.

**1759** British clockmaker John Harrison perfects an accurate, reliable marine chronometer that can be used to determine longitude at sea.

**1768–79** British sailor Captain James Cook undertakes three voyages of exploration, mainly in the Pacific and Southern Ocean.

**1770** Captain Cook and his crew discover the Great Barrier Reef on the eastern coast of Australia when their ship the *Endeavour* is almost wrecked on it.

**1770** American inventor and statesman Benjamin Franklin publishes the first map of the Gulf Stream.

**1805** British Admiral Francis Beaufort devises a scale for measuring and describing wind speed at sea.

**1819** Swiss chemist Alexander Marcet discovers that the basic chemistry of seawater is the same throughout the world.

**1831–36** British naturalist Charles Darwin conducts some of the earliest oceanographic research during the voyage of the HMS *Beagle*.

**1835** French physicist Gustave-Gaspard de Coriolis publishes a paper describing how ocean currents and moving air are affected by the spinning Earth. This becomes known as the Coriolis effect.

**1839–43** British navigator James Clark Ross commands an expedition to Antarctica, discovering the Ross Sea and the Ross Ice Shelf.

**1842** Darwin publishes his theory of the structure and formation of coral reefs and atolls. However, he is not proved right until the 1940s.

**1843** British naturalist Edward Forbes says that life cannot exist below 1,800 ft (550 m) in the oceans, starting a debate about the presence of an azoic (lifeless) zone.

**1868–69** During dredging operations from HMS *Lightning* and *Porcupine*, Scottish naturalist Wyville Thomson discovers oceanic life as deep as 14,403 ft (4,390 m). This disproves Edward Forbes' theory of a deep-ocean lifeless zone.

**1869** The Suez Canal between the Mediterranean and the Red Sea is completed after 11 years' work, but at the cost of at least 125,000 lives.

**1872** British scientist Sir William Thomson (Lord Kelvin) invents a sounding machine that uses wire cable to measure ocean depths. This is more accurate than older sounding methods using weighted hemp rope.

**1872–76** HMS *Challenger* makes the first thorough scientific exploration of the oceans. The ship travels 68,910 miles (110,900 km) on its four year voyage.

**1874–75** Charles Sigsbee of the US Navy pioneers new methods of mapping the ocean floor when surveying the Gulf of Mexico.

**1882** The first vessel specifically built as an oceanographic research vessel begins operations—the US Fish Commission steamer *Albatross*.

**1883** The volcano Krakatau erupts between Java and Sumatra, causing tsunamis that kill 36,000 people.

**1893–96** Norwegian explorer Fridtjof Nansen's ship *Fram* drifts over the central Arctic Ocean while locked in pack ice, demonstrating that the polar ice moves.

**1897** The first offshore oil rig is built off the coast of California, just 295 ft (90 m) from the shore.

**1900** The coastal town of Galveston, Texas, is destroyed by a hurricane. The storm surge and resulting floods kill more than 8,000 people.

**1903** Norwegian explorer Roald Amundsen leads the first expedition to traverse the Northwest Passage through the Arctic successfully.

**1912** The steamship *Titanic* sinks after colliding with an iceberg that has drifted 435 miles (700 km) southeast of Newfoundland; 1,500 people die in the mishap.

**1914** The Panama Canal between the Caribbean and the Pacific Ocean is opened after a lengthy construction project.

**1915** German meteorologist Alfred Wegener publishes his theory of continental drift, suggesting that all the continents were once joined together in a "supercontinent," one that he later calls Pangaea.

**1915** British explorer Ernest Shackleton's ship *Endurance* drifts 800 miles (1,300 km) while locked in the pack ice of the Antarctic Weddell Sea before being crushed and destroyed.

**1919** French scientists succeed in using an echo sounder (sonar) device to make the first depth measurements.

**1924** Russian biochemist Aleksander Oparin suggests that life on Earth could have originated in the oceans, as simple substances linked up to form the first complex molecules essential to life.

**1925–27** German survey ship *Meteor* uses sonar to produce a profile of the Mid-Atlantic Ridge.

**1934** US naturalist Charles Beebe and engineer Otis Barton make a world record descent of 3,028 ft (923 m) in a simple submersible called a bathysphere.

**1943** The first self-contained underwater breathing apparatus (SCUBA) is developed by French diver Jacques Cousteau and engineer Emile Gagnan.

**1948** US oceanographer Henry Melson Stommel publishes a paper explaining the workings of the Gulf Stream and the ocean circulation that redistributes heat around the world.

**1948** US marine geologists Bruce Heezen and Marie Tharp start using sonar data to map the features of the ocean floors. They publish their World Ocean Floor map in 1977.

**1954** Piloted by Georges Houot and Pierre Willm, the French research submersible *F.N.R.S. 3* dives to 13,255 ft (4,040 m) off the coast of Dakar, west Africa, pioneering a new era of manned submersibles.

**1955** The US survey ship *Pioneer* tows the first marine magnetometer and discovers magnetic "stripes" on the ocean floor off the West Coast of the US.

**1958** The American nuclear submarine USS *Nautilus* makes a voyage under the ice at the North Pole, proving that there is no land there.

**1959–62** US geologist Harry Hess proposes his theory of ocean-floor spreading from midocean ridges.

**1960** Jacques Piccard and Don Walsh descend into the deepest part of the Pacific—the Challenger Deep in the Mariana Trench—in the bathyscaphe *Trieste*.

**1961** The US Scripps Institution of Oceanography starts work on the Deep Tow System, pioneering remotely operated oceanographic research.

**1963** British scientists Frederick Vine and Drummond Matthews realize that magnetic stripes in the rocks of ocean floor provide proof of Hess's model of ocean-floor spreading.

**1963** A volcano erupts from the Mid-Atlantic Ridge just south of Iceland, and creates the new island of Surtsey.

**1963** Canadian geologist John Tuzo Wilson introduces the theory of hotspots, created in the Earth's crust by plumes of heat within the mantle.

**1963** First operational multibeam sonar sounding system installed on the American survey ship *Compass Island*.

**1964** The floor of the Pacific Ocean slides 65 ft (20 m) beneath Alaska, causing the most powerful earthquake ever recorded in North America.

**1964** The submersible *Alvin* makes its first dive. Operated by the Woods Hole Oceanographic Institution in the US, it ushers in a new age of intensive research and exploration in the deep oceans.

**1967** The La Rance tidal barrage begins operating near St. Malo, France, generating 240,000 kilowatts of electricity on each ebb tide.

**1968** The drilling ship *Glomar Challenger* takes samples of rocks up to 0.6 miles (1 km) below the ocean floor, and confirms the theory of ocean-floor spreading.

**1970** The worst tropical storm of the 20th century occurs in Bangladesh. High winds and flooding caused by the storm surge kill 300,000 to 500,000 people.

**1977** Scientists diving to the ocean floor in *Alvin* discover hydrothermal vents near the East Pacific Rise.

**1980** A single oil-well blowout from the *Ixtoc 1* drilling rig in the Bay of Campeche, Mexico, spills 525,000 tons (475,000 metric tons) of crude oil into the Gulf of Mexico.

**1982–83** An unusually severe El Niño event disrupts the weather throughout the Pacific region. Stocks of fish off Ecuador and Peru in the Eastern Pacific are virtually destroyed.

**1985** The dead zone in the Gulf of Mexico, caused by pollution carried into the sea by the Mississippi River, is systematically surveyed for the first time.

**1985** A team led by Dr. Robert Ballard discovers the wreck of the *Titanic* on the floor of the North Atlantic, 13,000 ft (4,000 m) below the ocean surface.

**1989** The giant oil tanker *Exxon Valdez* runs aground in Prince William Sound, Alaska, leaking 30 million gallons (114 million liters) of crude oil into the sea. The oil spill kills 250,000 seabirds and 6,000 sea otters and is the most destructive in history.

**1990** US geophysicist Syukuro Manabe uses a computer model of world climate to show that global warming could shut down the Gulf Stream.

**1995** The largest recorded ocean wave strikes the ocean liner *Queen Elizabeth II* off the coast of Newfoundland, Canada. The wave is 100 ft (30 m) high.

**1995** Using radar data from the Geosat satellite, Walter Smith and Dave Sandwell make the first truly accurate map of the ocean floor.

**1998** A major coral bleaching event caused by unusually high ocean water temperatures damages more than a quarter of the world's coral reefs.

**1998** Surveyors searching for oil fields discover a huge cold-water coral reef in the North Atlantic, off Scotland. The reef lies at a depth of 3,300 ft (1,000 m) and covers 39 sq miles (100 sq km).

**2000** The space probe *Galileo* provides evidence that Europa, one of Jupiter's moons, may have oceans of liquid water beneath its icy surface. If so, it would be the only other body in the solar system with oceans.

**2002** The Larsen B ice shelf on the northwest side of the Weddell Sea in Antarctica collapses because of high water temperatures. The collapse is widely blamed on global climate change.

**2003** The world's first open-sea tidal power generator is installed off the coast of north Devon in southern England. The system uses a turbine to harness the power of strong tidal streams.

**2004** Measurements of ocean currents associated with the Gulf Stream show that the flow has slowed by 30 percent since the 1960s. They suggest that the Gulf Stream may be under serious threat.

**2004** The Asian tsunami devastates coastal communities in the Indian Ocean. It causes more casualties than any other in recorded history, with more than 150,000 people killed and over 25,000 missing.

**2005** A storm surge caused by Hurricane Katrina floods the city of New Orleans , Louisiana, causing the deaths of more than 1,000 people.

**2005** An international team of oceanographers reports that the oceans are becoming dangerously acidified by carbon dioxide absorption from the air. This could have severe consequences for marine life.

**2006** Scientists drilling into ocean-floor sediments off Canada discover frozen methane at much shallower depths than expected, raising the possibility that it could be exploited as a fuel, and the fear that it might contribute to climate change.

**2006** A scientific study finds that fish stocks have collapsed in nearly one-third of sea fisheries, that the rate of decline is accelerating, and that if the trend continues, the oceans will be fished out by 2050.

**2007** Scientists report that the Southern Ocean is soaking up less carbon dioxide than in the past, and that this is accelerating climate change.

# GLOSSARY

**Abyssal plain** A flat area on the floor of the deep ocean, beyond the continental shelf, at a depth of 13,000–20,000 ft (4,000–6,000 m).

**Algae** Plantlike organisms that make sugar using the energy of sunlight. Seaweeds are large algae.

**Atmospheric pressure** The pressure created by the weight of air in the atmosphere, normally measured at sea level.

**Atoll** A ring-shaped island formed from a coral reef based on a sunken extinct volcano.

**Bacteria** Microscopic organisms with a simple single-celled structure. Some types can make food using energy that they get from sunlight or chemical reactions.

**Barrier reef** A coral reef that protects a shallow lagoon from the deep ocean.

**Basalt** A dark, heavy volcanic rock that forms oceanic crust and erupts as molten lava from midocean ridges and hotspot volcanoes.

**Bedrock** The solid rock that lies beneath more recent, softer sediments.

**Biogenic ooze** A soft sediment formed from the skeletal remains of microorganisms such as plankton.

**Black smoker** A hot spring or hydrothermal vent on the ocean floor, usually at a midocean ridge, that erupts dark, cloudy, mineral-rich water.

**Bycatch** Animals such as the wrong type of fish, marine mammals, and seabirds that are accidently caught when fishing.

**Carbohydrates** Compounds of carbon, hydrogen, and oxygen that store energy, made by some living things and used as food. Sugars are simple carbohydrates.

**Carbon dioxide** A gas that forms a very small percentage of the atmosphere. Living things such as plants and phytoplankton use it to make food, and it is also a greenhouse gas.

**Chemosynthesis** Using the energy of chemical reactions to make food (carbohydrates) from carbon dioxide and water.

**Chlorophyll** A substance that absorbs the energy of sunlight, used by some living things to make food in the process of photosynthesis.

**Coccolith** The skeleton of a microscopic marine organism called a coccolithophore, which in large numbers forms limestone or chalk rock.

**Condense** To turn from a gas to a liquid.

**Continental crust** A thick slab of relatively light rock that "floats" on the Earth's mantle.

**Continental rise** The slope that links the edge of the continental slope with the deep ocean floor.

**Continental shelf** The submerged fringe of a continent, which lies beneath a coastal sea.

**Continental slope** The edge of the continental shelf that slopes down to the continental rise and ocean floor.

**Convection** The movement and circulation of gases and liquids in response to heat.

**Convergent boundary** A boundary between two plates of the Earth's crust that are moving together, marked by earthquakes and volcanoes.

**Corals** Animals related to sea anemones that often form reef-building colonies.

**Crustacean** An animal with a hard, shell-like external skeleton and paired, jointed legs, such as a crab or shrimp.

**Current** A flow of ocean water, driven by the wind or by differences in water density caused by temperature and salt content.

**Cyclone** A weather system marked by clouds, rain, and strong winds, caused by air swirling into a region of rising warm, moist air.

**Dark zone** The deep region of the ocean where there is no light.

**Decompose** To rot.

**Delta** An accumulation of sand and silt laid down at the mouth of a river, usually with several distributary channels flowing over it.

**Density** The compactness of a substance. If the substance is squeezed together, it becomes more dense.

**Depression** An area of low atmospheric pressure in which warm air converges and rises. Also known as a cyclone.

**Divergent boundary** A boundary between two plates of the Earth's crust that are moving apart.

**DNA** (Deoxyribonucleic acid) The complex protein-like substance that contains the instructions needed to direct the growth of a living thing.

**Downwelling zone** A sea area where water is sinking.

**Echo-sounding** Using sound pulses (sonar) to measure water depth, or detect schools of fish.

**Ekman spiral** The way moving water swerves increasingly to the right or left with depth, so it moves in a different direction from the surface water.

**El Niño** A change in the ocean currents of the equatorial Pacific, when warm surface water moves east to suppress the normal flow of colder water. This affects the oceanic food supply and weather.

**Erosion** Wearing away, usually by natural forces such as waves on the shore.

**Estuary** A river mouth.

**Evaporate** To turn from a liquid to a gas.

**Food web** The complex relationship between living things that feed on each other.

**Fossil fuel** A carbon compound that can be burned to release energy, such as coal, oil, or natural gas, made by the decomposition of dead organisms over millions of years.

**Fringing reef** A coral reef that lies along a rocky shoreline (continent or island), and does not enclose a well-developed shallow lagoon.

**Geyser** A jet of hot water and steam that regularly erupts from volcanically heated rocks.

**Glacier** A mass of ice that is flowing very slowly downhill, usually through a deep valley.

**Global conveyor** The linked system of currents that carries ocean water around the globe.

**Granite** A crystalline, hard rock that is one of the main rocks found in continental crust.

**Greenhouse effect** The warming effect caused by the way atmospheric gases such as carbon dioxide, methane, and water vapor absorb some of the heat radiated from Earth, and stop it from escaping into space.

**Gyre** A large-scale circular pattern of ocean currents, rotating clockwise north of the equator, and counterclockwise south of the equator.

**Headland** A narrow area of coastal land projecting between two bays.

**Hotspot** An unusually hot part of the Earth's thick mantle, which makes volcanoes erupt through the crust above.

**Hydrothermal vent** A hot spring in the ocean floor, normally on a spreading rift. Also known as a black smoker.

**Intertidal** Refers to the area of the shore that is covered and uncovered by the tides.

**Invertebrate** An animal that does not have an internal skeleton based on spinal bones.

**Island arc** A line of islands marking a boundary between two plates of the Earth's crust, created by volcanic activity as one plate plunges beneath the other and is destroyed.

**Krill** Oceanic shrimp that form large swarms in the Southern Ocean, and are the main food of most Antarctic animals.

**Lagoon** An area of shallow water that has been cut off from the sea.

**Lava** Molten rock that erupts from volcanoes or volcanic fissures.

**Longline** A very long fishing line equipped with thousands of baited hooks.

**Longshore drift** The movement of beach material along the shore by waves.

**Magma** Molten rock that has not erupted and is still contained within the Earth's crust.

**Mangrove** A type of tree that grows in tidal water in the tropics, or a forest of these trees.

**Mantle** The thick layer of very hot, but not molten, rock beneath the Earth's crust.

**Mantle plume** A rising current of heat within the Earth's mantle.

**Maritime climate** A climate that is strongly influenced by a nearby ocean. It has cool summers and mild winters, and regular rain.

**Meltwater** Water that flows off melting ice.

**Methane** A gas formed from carbon and hydrogen, that is both a fossil fuel (natural gas) and a potent greenhouse gas.

**Microbe** A microscopic living thing.

**Midocean ridge** A ridge of submarine mountains on the ocean floor, created by a spreading rift between two plates of the Earth's crust.

**Migration** A regular journey by an animal, often seasonal, made to exploit temporary food resources or good breeding conditions.

**Minerals** The natural materials that make up rocks. They are carried in ocean water, and many are used as nutrients by oceanic phytoplankton.

**Molecule** The smallest particle of a substance such as a gas or liquid, formed from atoms of the elements that make up that substance. A water molecule, for example, contains two hydrogen atoms and one oxygen atom.

**Mollusk** A soft-bodied animal that may have a shell, such as a snail or a clam. An octopus is an advanced type of mollusk.

**Monsoon** A seasonal wind change that alters the weather pattern, especially in southern Asia.

**Neap tide** A twice-monthly tide with a small tidal range between high and low water.

**Nutrients** Substances that living things need to build their tissues.

**Ocean trench** A deep chasm in the ocean floor created by one plate of the Earth's crust being dragged beneath another.

**Oceanic crust** The relatively thin crust of solid basalt that lies above the Earth's mantle and forms the bedrock of the ocean floor.

**Organism** A living thing.

**Parasite** An organism that feeds off other live organisms.

**Photophore** A living organ that produces light.

**Photosynthesis** The process by which green plants and some other organisms use the energy of light to make carbohydrate food (sugar) from carbon dioxide and water.

**Phytoplankton** Microscopic organisms that drift near the ocean surface and make food by photosynthesis.

**Pillow lava** Pillow-shaped lumps of volcanic rock, usually basalt, formed by lava erupting from the ocean floor and solidifying in the cold water.

**Plankton** Living things that mainly drift in the water, rather than swimming actively.

**Plankton bloom** An increase in the amount of plankton in water, caused by the organisms multiplying rapidly.

**Predator** An animal that preys upon other live animals, attacking and eating them.

**Prevailing wind** A wind that blows from a particular direction most of the time.

**Protein** A complex substance that a living thing makes out of simpler nutrients and uses to form its tissues.

**Protozoan** A very simple type of animal, usually microscopic.

**Reef** A ridge of submerged rock, often created by marine animals called corals.

**Rift** A break in the Earth's crust caused by the rocks moving apart.

**ROV** A remotely operated vehicle or nonmanned submersible.

**Salt marsh** A marshy area fringing a tidal zone such as a river estuary.

**Scavenger** An animal that eats the remains of dead animals.

**Scuba** An air-supply system used by divers. The word SCUBA stands for Self-Contained Underwater Breathing Apparatus.

**Seamount** An ocean-floor volcano that does not break the ocean surface to form an island.

**Sediment** Solid particles such as sand, silt, or mud that have settled on the seabed or elsewhere. They may harden to form sedimentary rock.

**Silica** A compound of silicon and oxygen that forms the mineral quartz, the main ingredient of sand, and is used to make glass.

**Sonar** A system that uses pulses of sound waves to detect solid objects.

**Sounding** Finding the depth of water.

**Spawn** To release eggs into the water, where they may be fertilized. Most fish reproduce like this.

**Spring tide** A twice-monthly tide with a large tidal range between high and low water.

**Storm surge** A local, temporary rise in sea level caused by storm winds and low air pressure.

**Strait** A narrow stretch of water between two coasts.

**Subduction zone** A boundary between two plates of the Earth's crust, where one plate plunges beneath the other and is destroyed.

**Submarine fan** A fan-shaped area of sediment on the seafloor, formed by river water flowing into the sea.

**Submersible** A craft designed to dive to the ocean depths.

**Sunlit zone** The region of the ocean near the surface, with enough sunlight for phytoplankton and seaweeds to make food and grow.

**Supercontinent** A large landmass formed by several continents becoming joined together.

**Superheated** Heated above the normal boiling point at which a liquid would turn into a gas under conditions of high pressure.

**Swell** A regular wave pattern.

**Temperate** Neither tropical nor polar.

**Thermocline** The boundary between deep, cold, dense water and a layer of warmer, less dense water that floats at the surface.

**Thermohaline circulation** A global flow of ocean currents, driven by variations in water density caused by differences of temperature and salt content.

**Tidal race** A fast-moving tidal stream that has chaotic waves and whirlpools.

**Tidal range** The difference between high and low tide level.

**Tidal stream** A horizontal flow of water created by the rise and fall of the tide.

**Trade winds** Steady winds that blow from the east in the tropical oceans.

**Transform boundary** A boundary between two plates of the Earth's crust, where one plate is sliding against the other.

**Tsunami** A destructive sea wave usually produced by an earthquake, but which can also be caused by submarine landslides or volcanic eruptions.

**Turbidity current** An underwater flow of water loaded with mud and other sediments, resembling a river in flood.

**Twilight zone** The deep region of the ocean where only faint blue light penetrates from the surface.

**Upwelling zone** A part of the ocean where deep water that is rich in plant nutrients is drawn up to the surface.

**Water vapor** The gas formed when liquid water is warmed and evaporates.

**Wavelength** Distance between two wave crests.

**Zooplankton** The community of mostly small animals that drift and swim in the ocean, mainly near the surface.

**Zooxanthellae** Microscopic organisms that live in the tissues of coral and other marine animals, and make food by photosynthesis.

# INDEX

A page number in **bold** refers to the main entry for that subject.

# N



# O



# P



# R



# S



# T



# UV



# W

# ACKNOWLEDGMENTS

**Dorling Kindersley** would like to thank Margaret Parrish for Americanization.



**Picture Credits**
The publisher would like to thank the following for their kind permission to reproduce their photographs:

**Abbreviations key:**
a-above, b-below/bottom, c-center, f-far, l-left, r-right, t-top

1 DK Images: David Peart. 7 Marie Tharp: Marie Tharp 1977/2003. Reproduced by permission of Marie Tharp Oceanographic Cartographer, One Washington Ave.., South Nyack, New York 10960 (tr). 8 NASA / JPL-Caltech: (bl). NASA: JPL (cl). Science Photo Library: (tl). 9 Corbis: Bruce DeBoer (br). DK Images: David Peart (c). 10 Ancient Art & Architecture Collection: (bl). The Bridgeman Art Library: Villa Farnese, Caprarola, Lazio, Italy (br). DK Images: Statens Historiska Museum, Stockholm (t). 11 National Maritime Museum, London: (br) (tl) (tr). 12 The Bridgeman Art Library: Down House, Kent (tl). DK Images: Natural History Museum, London (cl). Miriam Sayago Gil, Spanish Institute of Oceanography (Malaga) : (bl). 12-13 Japan Agency for Marine-Earth Science and Technology (JAMSTEC) : IODP (c). 13 Science Photo Library: Dr. Ken MacDonald (tr); Planetary Visions Ltd. (br). 14 Corbis: Ralph White (bl). Mary Evans Picture Library: (tc). Woods Hole Oceanographic Instititution: WHOIalvinrecoverysd (cl). 15 Getty Images: Paul Nicklen/National Geographic (cr). 16 Science Photo Library: W. Haxby, Lamont-Doherty Earth Observatory (cra) (tr); SPL (br); US Geological Survey (cr). 17 Marie Tharp: Heezen & Tharp are perusing a film transparency of their diagram, photo by Robert Brunke, 1968. Marie Tharp 1977/2003. Reproduced by permission of Marie Tharp Oceanographic Cartographer, One Washington Ave., South Nyack, New York 10960 (tl). World Ocean Floor Panorama by Bruce C.Heezen & Marie Tharp, 1977. Marie Tharp 1977/2003. Reproduced by permission of Marie Tharp Oceanographic Cartographer, One Washington Ave., South Nyack, New York 10960 (tr). 18 DK Images: Natural History Museum, London (br). 18-19 DK Images: Satellite Imagemap Copyright © 1996-2003 Planetary Visions (c/Earth cross section). 20 Science Photo Library: Dr. Steve Gull & Dr. John Fielden (br). Marie Tharp: World Ocean Floor Panorama by Bruce C.Heezen & Marie Tharp, 1977. Marie Tharp 1977/2003. Reproduced by permission of Marie Tharp Oceanographic Cartographer, One Washington Ave., South Nyack, New York 10960 (bl). 21 Science Photo Library: Dr. Ken MacDonald (cl); B. Murton/Southampton Oceanography Center (tr); OAR/National Undersea Research Program (tl). 22 Getty Images: AFP (bl). NASA: Jacques Descloitres, MODIS Rapid Response Team (cr). 23 DK Images: Rowan Greenwood (tr); Katy Williamson (tl). Photoshot / NHPA: Martin Harvey (tc). Science Photo Library: Dr. Ken MacDonald (cr); Alexis Rosenfeld (b). 24 DK Images: Sean Hunter (br). NASA: Jacques Descloitres, MODIS Rapid Response Team (bl). Science Photo Library: US Geological Survey (tl). 25 Corbis: Michael S. Yamashita (tl). Getty Images: AFP (b). Science Photo Library: Planetary Visions Ltd. (tr). 26 Science Photo Library: Ken M. Johns (l). 27 Brian M. Guzzetti from the far corners photography: (bl). NOAA: (br). PA Photos: Gemunu Amarasinghe/AP (t). 28 Alamy Images: George & Monserrate Schwarz (tl). Science Photo Library: John Heseltine (bc). 29 Corbis: Larry Dale Gordon/zefa (tl); Jason Hawkes (tc); Jim Sugar (tr). Panos Pictures: Jeremy Horner (b). 30-31 Alamy Images: James Symington (b). 31 NASA: Jacques Descloitres, MODIS Rapid Response Team (t). Science Photo Library: Jan Hinsch (c); Dirk Wiersma (br). 32 Science Photo Library: Steve Gschmeissner (tr); Sinclair Stammers (cl). 33 Alamy Images: A Room With Views (cr). DK Images: CONACULTA-INAH-MEX (t). 34 Alamy Images: Blickwinkel (tl). DK Images: Katy Williamson (cl/glacial lagoon). 35 NASA: (tl). Photoshot / NHPA: Linda Pitkin (tr). Robert Harding Picture Library: Richard Ainsworth (br). 36 NASA: (b); MODIS Instrument Team, NASA, GSFC (c). 37 Corbis: Amos Nachoum (bc). Still Pictures: Kelvin Aitken (r). 38 Bryan and Cherry Alexander Photography: (clb). NOAA: Michael van Woert, NOAA NESDIS, ORA (cl). Courtesy of Don Perovich: (bl). popperfoto.com: (cr). 38-39 Bryan and Cherry Alexander Photography. 39 Getty Images: Photographer's Choice/Siegfried Layda (br). 41 Alamy Images: Michael Diggin (b); David Tipling (cl). DK Images: Rough Guides (tl). FLPA: Frans Lanting/ Minden (c). Kos Picture Source: Bob Grieser (tr). 42 Getty Images: Arnulf Husmo (bl). 42-43 NASA: Jeff Schmaltz. NASA, GSFC. 43 Science Photo Library: J.B. Golden (tl). 44 Alamy Images: David Gregs (clb). OSF: (tl). 45 Corbis: Bryn Colton/Assignments Photographers (bl). Getty Images: Taxi/Helena Vallis (t). Miriam Sayago Gil, Spanish Institute of Oceanography (Malaga) : (cr). 46 Alamy Images: Bert de Ruiter (c). 47 Alamy Images: Bill Brooks (tl). Still Pictures: Markus Dlouny (br). 48 Science Photo Library: NASA (tl). 49 NASA: Courtesy SeaWIFS Project, NASA, GSFC & ORBIMAGE (bl). 50 Splashdowndirect.com: (b). 51 FLPA: Chris Newbert/ Minden Pictures (bl). Science Photo Library: R.B. Husar/NASA (tl). 52 Corbis: Galen Rowell (l). 53 Corbis: Paul Souders (r). Science Photo Library: Chris Sattlberger (cl). 54 Corbis: Clouds Hill Imaging Ltd. (tl); Lawson Wood (c). Science Photo Library: NASA (br). 55 Corbis: Ralph A. Clevenger (tr); Douglas P. Wilson; Frank Lane Picture Agency (tc). Science Photo Library: Steve Gschmeissner (tc/ Phytoplankton). 56 Corbis: Einrich Baesemann/dpa (br); Visuals Unlimited (tl). 57 Ardea: Ron & Valerie Taylor (tl). Corbis: Amos Nachoum (tr); Denis Scott (cl). 58 Corbis: Rick Price (clb); Jeffrey L. Rotman (crb). DK Images: David Peart (br). Science Photo Library: Nancy Sefton (bl). 59 Corbis: Jeffrey L. Roman (cra); Jeffrey L. Rotman (br); Denis Scott (bc). FLPA: Norbert Wu/Minden Pictures (cr). 60 OSF: (t). Science Photo Library: Dr. Gene Feldman, NASA GSFC (cr). 61 Alamy Images: Alaska Stock LLC (cl). DK Images: Rough Guides (tl). 62 OSF: Roger Jackman (br). Sue Scott: (bl). 63 Corbis: Roger Tidman (cl). DK Images: Natural History Museum, London (fclb); David Peart (fcrb); Rough Guides (crb). FLPA: David Hosking (tr). 64 Corbis: Staffan Widstrand (t). FLPA: Flip Nicklin/Minden Pictures (br). Science Photo Library: Dr. Gene Feldman, NASA GSFC (cr). 65 Corbis: Dan Guravich (c); Rick Price (tl). DK Images: Toronto Zoo (br). FLPA: Norbert Wu/Minden Pictures (tr). 66 DK Images: David Peart (tl). 67 Alamy Images: Image State (tl). Corbis: Bruno Levy/zefa (bl). FLPA: Norbert Wu/Minden Pictures (br). Getty Images: Photographer's Choice/ Peter Pinnock (tr). Science Photo Library: Rudiger Lehnen (cra). 68 Alamy Images: Image State (b). Corbis: Owen Franken (tr). Science Photo Library: Dr. Gene Feldman, NASA GSFC (cl). 69 Alamy Images: Michael Patrick O'Neill (c); Stephen Frink Collection (tl). OSF: (bl). 70 Corbis: Jeffrey L. Rotman (cr). 71 Image Quest 3-D: Peter Batson (bl); Peter Herring (br) (tl) (tr). 72 Corbis: Ralph White (l) (cr). DeepSeaPhotography.Com: Peter Batson (br). 73 Monika Bright, University of Vienna, Austria: (tr). DeepSeaPhotography.Com: Peter Batson (tl). NOAA: Ocean Explorer (bl). Science Photo Library: T. Stevens & P. McKinley, Pacific Northwest Laboratory (bc). 74 Corbis: Yann Arthus-Bertrand (br). 75 Corbis: Ralph White (bl). DK Images: Natural History Museum, London (cl). FLPA: Norbert Wu/Minden Pictures (t). 76 Alamy Images: Dalgleish Images (tl). Ecoscene: Sue Anderson (cr); Jim Winkley (b). 77 Marine Current Turbines Ltd.: (tl). Copyright SkySails: (bl). Still Pictures: Godard (r). 78 Corbis: Natalie Forbes (bl) (br). 79 Corbis: Michael S. Lewis (br); Chaiwat Subprasom/Reuters (tl). Still Pictures: Larbi (tr); Jim Wark (cr). 80 DeepSeaPhotography.Com: Kim Westerkov (br). Ecoscene: Quentin Bates (l). 81 Ardea: Valerie Taylor (bl). DK Images: David Peart (tr). Ecoscene: Tom Ennis (br). OSF: (tc). 82 Corbis: Dean Conger (c). Still Pictures: Glueckstadt (tr); Hartmut Schwarzbach (br). 83 Alamy Images: FAN Travelstock (c). DK Images: Angus Beare (tr). 84 Alamy Images: Arco Images (br). Corbis: Joe Haresh/epa (cl). Science Photo Library: Bill Backman (l). Still Pictures: BIOS Crocetta Tony (cr); Robert Book (c). 85 Ecoscene: John Liddiard (bl); Sally Morgan (br). NASA: (t). 86 Getty Images: Hans Strand (bl). NASA: Finley Holiday Films (tr). 87 Alamy Images: Michael Foyle (br). DK Images: David Peart (cra). NASA: MODIS, GSFC (tl). Science Photo Library: Matthew Oldfield, Subazoo (c). 88 Corbis: Niall Benvie (cl). Save The Albatross Campaign: Photo by Jim Enticott (b). 88-89 DK Images: David Peart (c). 89 Alamy Images: Craig Steven Thrasher (tr). Still Pictures: Fred Bruemmer (bl). 90-91 Alamy Images: Comstock Images (page margins). 92-93 Alamy Images: Comstock Images (page margins).

**Jacket images:**
**Front:** Corbis: Jeffrey L. Rotman. **Back:** Corbis: Stephen Frink fcr; Stuart Westmorland cl; Getty Images: Science Faction/Stuart Westmorland fcl; Taxi/Peter David cr. **Spine:** Corbis: Jeffrey L. Rotman